# INCIDENTAL
# INVENTIONS

# Elena Ferrante
# Incidental Inventions

*Translated from the Italian by*
ANN GOLDSTEIN

*Illustrations by*
ANDREA UCINI

Europa
*editions*

Europa Editions
214 West 29th Street
New York, N.Y. 10001
www.europaeditions.com
info@europaeditions.com

Translated by Ann Goldstein, the pieces included in this volume,
with the exception of "Collisions," were originally published  over the course
of 2018 in the *Guardian*.

Translation by Ann Goldstein
Original title: *L'invenzione occasionale*

Library of Congress Cataloging in Publication Data is available
ISBN 978-1-60945-558-3

Illustrations by Andrea Ucini

Book design by Emanuele Ragnisco
www.mekkanografici.com

Printed in Italy, at Puntoweb

# Contents

# Collisions

In the autumn of 2017 the *Guardian* proposed that I write a weekly column. I was flattered and at the same time frightened. I had no experience with that type of writing, and I was afraid that I wouldn't be able to do it. After much hesitation, I told the editors that I would accept the offer if they would send me a series of questions, which I would answer, each time, within the limits of the allotted space. My request was immediately granted, along with an agreement that the column wouldn't last more than a year. The year passed slowly, and it was instructive for me. I had never put myself in the situation of being obliged to write, locked within an invulnerable perimeter, on topics that I myself had asked the extremely patient editors to suggest. I'm used to looking on my own for a story, characters, a logic, putting one word after another, often laboriously, eliminating a lot; what I find at the end—assuming that I find something—is surprising, especially to me. It's as if one sentence had generated the next, taking advantage of my still uncertain intentions, and I never know if the result is good or not: yet it's there, and now I have to work on it—the moment has come when the text will take the form I want.

But the *Guardian* columns were governed by the random collision between the editors' subject and the urgency of writing. While the first draft of a story might be followed immediately by a long—sometimes very long—period of closer examination, rewriting, expansion or meticulous reduction, here the process was minimal. For these pieces I rummaged through memory in search of small illustrative experiences; impulsively drew on convictions formed by books read many years ago, then cast off and recovered, thanks to other readings; pursued sudden intuitions inspired by that same need to write; came to abrupt conclusions because the space had been used up. In other words, it was a new form of writing: every time I hurriedly dipped the bucket into some dark depth of my mind, I hauled up a sentence and waited apprehensively for others to follow.

The result is this book, which happens to begin on 20 January 2018, with the perennial uncertainty of something done for the first time, and happens to end on 12 January 2019, with the clarity of something done for the last time. I was tempted to give a more thoughtful order to the different parts, and I drafted possible arrangements. But setting them out as if they had originated in a carefully considered project seemed an exaggeration, and in the end I left them in the order of publication. I didn't want to hide—especially from myself—their nature as incidental inventions, no different from those with which we daily react to the world we happen to live in.

# The Pieces

# The First Time

*20 January 2018*

Some time ago, I planned to describe my first times. I listed a certain number of them: the first time I saw the sea, the first time I flew in an aeroplane, the first time I got drunk, the first time I fell in love, the first time I made love. It was an exercise both arduous and pointless.

For that matter, how could it be otherwise? We always look at first times with excessive indulgence. Even if by their nature they're founded on inexperience, and so as a rule are not very successful, we recall them with sympathy, with regret. They're swallowed up by all the times that have followed, by their transformation into habit, and yet we attribute to them the power of the unrepeatable.

Precisely because of this innate contradiction, my project began to sink right away and shipwrecked conclusively when I tried to describe my first love truthfully. I made an effort to search my memory for details and I found few. He was very tall, very thin, and seemed handsome to me. He was seventeen, I fifteen. We saw each other every day at six in the evening. We went to a deserted alley behind the bus station. He spoke to me, but not much; kissed me, but not much; caressed me, but not much. What primarily interested him was that I should caress him. One evening—was it evening?—I kissed him as I would have liked him to kiss me. I did it with such an eager, shameless intensity that afterwards I decided not to see him again. But already I don't know if that really happened then, or in the course of other brief loves that followed. Certainly I loved that boy to the point where, seeing him, I lost every perception of the world, and felt close to fainting, not out of weakness but out of an excess of energy.

Consequently, I discovered, what I distinctly remember of my first love is my state of confusion. Or rather, the more I worked on it, the more I focused on deficiencies: vague memory, sentimental uncertainties, anxieties, dissatisfaction. Nothing, in fact, was sufficient; I expected and wanted more, and was surprised that he, on the other hand, after wanting me so much, found me superfluous and ran away because he had other things to do.

All right, I said to myself, you will write about how altogether wanting first love is. But, as soon as I tried, the writing rebelled, it tended to fill gaps, to give the experience the stereotypical melancholy of adolescence. It's why I said, that's enough of first times. What we were at the beginning is only a vague patch of colour contemplated from the edge of what we have become.

# Fears

*27 January 2018*

I'm not brave. Most of all I'm afraid of anything that creeps, and especially snakes. I'm afraid of spiders, woodworms, mosquitoes, even flies. I'm afraid of heights, and of elevators, cable cars, aeroplanes. I'm afraid of the very ground we stand on when I imagine that it might split open or, because of a sudden breakdown in the workings of the universe, fall down, as in the nursery rhyme we recited as children, playing ring around the rosy. *Ring around the rosy, The world falls down, The earth falls down, All fall down*: ah, how those words terrified me. I'm afraid of all human beings when they become violent: I'm afraid of them when they shout, when they insult, when they wield words of contempt, clubs, chains, weapons that slash or shoot, atomic bombs.

And yet, as a child, whenever it was necessary to appear fearless, I appeared fearless. I soon got used to being less afraid of dangers, whether real or imaginary, and began to fear more, much more, the moment when others reacted as I hadn't known how to react. My girlfriends shrieked because there was a spider? I overcame my disgust and killed it. The man I loved proposed a vacation in the mountains with the obligatory rides on a chairlift? I was dripping with sweat, but I went.

Once, the cat brought in a snake and left it under my bed, and I, with a broom and dustpan, screaming, chased it out. And if someone threatens my daughters, or me, or any human being, or any harmless animal, I resist the desire to run away.

Popular opinion has it that people who react as stubbornly as I've trained myself to have real courage, which consists precisely in overcoming fear. But I don't agree. We fearful belligerents place at the top of all our fears the fear of losing self-respect. We value ourselves very highly, and in order not to have to face our own humiliation, we are capable of anything. In other words, we drive away our fears not out of altruism but out of egotism.

And so, I have to admit, I'm afraid of myself. I've known for a long time now that I can get carried away, so I'm trying to soften the aggressive reactions I've forced myself to have ever since I was a child. I'm learning, like a character in Conrad, to accept fear, even to exhibit it with self-mockery. I began to do this when I realised that my daughters got scared if I defended them from dangers—small, large or imaginary—with excessive ardour. What perhaps should be feared most is the fury of frightened people.

## Keeping a Diary                    *3 February 2018*

I kept a diary for several years as a girl. I was a timid adolescent; all I said was yes, and mostly I was silent. In my diary, on the other hand, I let go: I recounted in detail what happened to me every day, very secret events, bold thoughts. So I was really worried about it: I was afraid that my family, especially my mother, would find it and read it. Thus I was always inventing safe hiding places that soon seemed to me unsafe.

Why was I worried? Because if, in everyday life, I was so embarrassed, so cautious, that I scarcely breathed, the diary produced in me a craving for truth. I thought that when one writes, it makes no sense to be contained, to censor oneself, and as a result I wrote mostly—maybe only—about what I would have preferred to be silent about, resorting among other things to a vocabulary that I would never have dared to use in speaking.

This soon created a situation that exhausted me. On the one hand,

I made an effort of expression every day to demonstrate to myself that I was ruthlessly honest, and that nothing would ever prevent me from being so; on the other, I was terrified that someone might set eyes on my pages.

That contradiction was with me for a long time, and in many ways it's still alive today. If I chose to make visible in writing what, if I hadn't written, would have remained completely hidden in my head, why then was I anxious that my diary might be discovered?

Around the age of twenty, it seemed to me I'd found a solution that satisfied me. I had to stop writing my diary and channel the desire to tell the truth—my most unutterable truths—into an invented story. I took that route partly because the diary itself was starting to become fiction. Very often, for example, I didn't have time to write every day, and as a result it seemed to me that the thread of causes and effects was broken. So I filled the voids by writing pages that I later back-dated. And in doing so I gave the facts, the reflections a coherence that didn't always exist in the pages that I wrote daily. So it was probably the experience of the diary and its contradictions that transformed me into a fiction writer. In the invented stories, I felt that I was—I and my truths—a little safer.

In fact, as soon as that new writing gained ground, I threw away my diaries. I did it because the writing seemed crude, without worthwhile thoughts, full of childish exaggerations and, above all, far removed from how I now remembered my adolescence. Since then, I've no longer felt the need to keep a diary.

# The End

*10 February 2018*

More and more often I hear my friends say: it's not death that scares me but illness. And I, too, repeat the phrase. When I try to unpack it to understand it a little better, I discover that for me it means: I'm frightened not by the idea of ceasing to exist, but by the invasiveness of treatments, by the oscillation between the illusion of recovery and disappointment, by death throes. It's as if I were confessing that what truly worries me is the end of good health, along with everything that that entails: debilitation, progressive inactivity, pleasure diminished to the simple assertion that I am still "I," and that for now, somehow or other, I'm still alive.

As a result, the idea of death itself seems increasingly pallid. What is terrifying, instead, is the end of enjoyable life, of a full life. And for me that's because the belief in some kind of beyond, acquired during childhood, has faded over time.

When I was a child, my grandmother was the most active person in the house; then she had a stroke and was paralysed for years. She sat in a corner of the kitchen and I, as a girl, didn't experience her suffering and humiliation, nor did she signal it to me, even with her eyes, as something intolerable. Death came suddenly, and I grieved within the religious framework in which I'd been raised. Death meant that she had gone away, leaving a body reduced to a cold, rigid thing. Her dying had very precise features: I felt it as a terrifying immobility and a very mysterious movement. My grandmother had crossed over into an elsewhere.

Later, every form of religious belief seemed absurd to me, and death was as if disfigured. The immobility remained, the movement vanished. The dead body became simply the sign of the end of life in a specific individual. Today I would never say: he has gone away. I've lost the sense of the crossing over: nothing goes up to heaven, we don't move to another world, we don't return, we aren't reborn. We remain definitively immobile; death is the last point on the segment of life that has chanced to be ours.

Thus my attention, like that of many others, is concentrated not on dying but on living poorly. We hope that life is as long as possible, and yet that it will end conclusively when we have declined to the point where no treatment can make it tolerable. I don't know which is better: this adult belief or the belief I maintained until adolescence. Beliefs aren't good or bad; they serve only to bring order, at least momentarily, to our anguish.

## The False and the True

*17 February 2018*

I can't trace a line of separation between fiction and nonfiction. Let's say I have an idea for a story in which, at the age of forty-eight, in an empty country house in winter, I am locked in the shower cubicle, I can't turn the water off, the hot water is used up. Did that really happen to me? No. Did it happen to a person I know? Yes. Was that person forty-eight? No.

Why then do I construct a story in the first person, as if it had happened to me? Why do I say it was winter when, in fact, it was summer, why do I say the hot water was used up when it wasn't, why do I make the woman's imprisonment last for hours, when the actual person got out in five minutes, why do I complicate the story with many other events, with feelings, anxieties, frightened reflections, when the event recounted is a small, unimportant episode? Because—I could answer—I am trying to make fiction by following a course that Gogol summarised like this: Give me any small everyday event and I will make a five-act play.

But I don't intend to answer like that. I want to offer the opposite example. I'm tired of fiction; I no longer see a reason to go hunting for anecdotes from which to make five-act plays. So I talk to my friend who was locked in the shower for a few minutes with the intention of recounting faithfully what happened. I go there with my iPad and I even make a video; I want to stick as closely to the facts as possible.

Then I go home and set to work. I read and reread my notes, I look again and again at the video, I listen over and over: and I'm baffled. Why does my friend get muddled when she talks about the defective cubicle? Why are the first well-considered sentences followed by faulty clauses, an accentuation of the dialectal cadence? Why, when she reports to me her trivial experience, does she look insistently to the right? What is there on the right that I can't see in the recording and didn't see in reality? How will I work when I move on to the writing? Will I clean up that language? Will I imitate her confusion? Will I lessen the confusion in order to minimise it, will I exaggerate it to make it very obvious? Will I try to hypothesise what's hidden on the right? And what if nothing is hidden?

In other words, my effort at faithfulness cannot be separated from the search for coherence, the imposition of order and meaning, even the imitation of the lack of order and meaning. Because writing is innately artificial, its every use involves some form of fiction. The dividing line is rather, as Virginia Woolf said, how much truth the fiction inherent in writing is able to capture.

# Linguistic Nationality                    *24 February 2018*

I love my country, but I have no patriotic spirit and no national pride. What's more, I digest pizza poorly, I eat very little spaghetti, I don't speak in a loud voice, I don't gesticulate, I hate all mafias, I don't exclaim "Mamma mia!" National characteristics are simplifications that should be contested. Being Italian, for me, begins and ends with the fact that I speak and write in the Italian language.

Put that way it doesn't seem like much, but really it's a lot. A language is a compendium of the history, geography, material and spiritual life, the vices and virtues, not only of those who speak it, but also of those who have spoken it through the centuries. The words, the grammar, the syntax are a chisel that shapes our thought. Not to mention our literary tradition, an extraordinary refinery of raw experience that has been active for centuries and centuries, a reservoir of intelligence and expressive techniques; it's the tradition that has formed me, and on which I'm proud to have drawn.

When I say that I'm Italian because I write in Italian, I mean that I'm fully Italian—but Italian in the only way that I'm willing to attribute to myself a nationality. I don't like the other ways; they frighten me, especially when they become nationalism, chauvinism, imperialism and reprehensibly use language to wall themselves in, either by cultivating a purity as pointless as it is impossible, or by imposing language through overwhelming economic power and weapons. It has happened, it happens, it will happen, and it's an evil that tends to cancel out differences and therefore impoverishes us all.

I prefer linguistic nationality as a point of departure for dialogue, an effort to cross over the limit, to look beyond the border—beyond all borders, especially those of gender. Thus my only heroes are translators (I especially love those who are experts in the art of simultaneous translation). I love them in particular when they're also passionate readers and propose translations themselves. Thanks to them, Italianness travels through the world, enriching it, and the world, with its many languages, passes through Italianness and modifies it. Translators transport nations into other nations; they are the first to reckon with distant modes of feeling. Even their mistakes are evidence of a positive force. Translation is our salvation: it draws us out of the well in which, entirely by chance, we are born.

I am therefore Italian, completely and with pride. But if I could, I would descend into all languages and let myself be permeated by them all. Even the terrible Google Translate consoles me. We can be much more than what we happen to be.

# Laughter

*3 March 2018*

I laugh willingly, without restraint, and so hard that the muscles around my mouth ache. I also like to make people laugh, but I'm not too successful at it; in general what seems comic to me doesn't make anyone else laugh.

I remember a design that was very amusing to me as a girl. You have to imagine the sign that prohibits honking: a trumpet in a circle, crossed out by a diagonal strip. Next to it is a convertible, and a slow-moving pedestrian who keeps the car from proceeding. The driver is leaning out over the windshield and playing the violin in the pedestrian's ear. I laughed, and my girlfriends said: "Why do you find it so funny?"

Yes, why? It's still not clear to me. I like the humour that derives from situations like this, and I get on well with anyone who can come up with this type of idea.

Maybe I laugh because the symbol of the trumpet is taken literally:

honking the horn is prohibited, playing the violin evidently is not, and so it becomes the bow's job to signal to the pedestrian that he'd better move. Maybe I laugh because it seems to me that resorting to the violin doesn't simply get around the prohibition, but suggests replacing the extremely annoying horn with something more delicate. Maybe I laugh because bans have always made me anxious, and a polite violation, almost a non-violation, relaxes the tension.

Laughter for me can do only this: stretch what is tense to the point where it is unendurable. Otherwise it seems to me overrated. I've never believed that laughter is able to put an end to the injustices of the world. No power has ever yielded an inch thanks to a laugh. Ridicule, yes, annoys the powerful, but it doesn't bury them. Yet for the moment we're laughing, we feel their grip on our life relax a little. Laughter is a short, very short, sigh of relief.

That must be why the laughter that interests me most, in the context of a story, is incongruous laughter, the laughter that explodes in situations where laughing is inconceivable, in fact seems an enormity. There is a moment like this in Stanisław Lem's *His Master's Voice*: a nine-year-old child, confronted by the unendurable death agony of his mother, goes off into his room, makes faces in the mirror, and laughs. That laughter in the face of the unendurable is risky for literature, and it's the laughter that interests me most.

# Pregnant

*10 March 2018*

I was a terrible mother, a great mother. Pregnancy changes everything: our body, our feelings, the hierarchical order of our lives. The convention by which we have always considered ourselves one and indivisible fails. Now we have two hearts, all our organs are duplicated, our sex is doubled—we are female plus female or female plus male. And we are divisible, not metaphorically but in the acute reality of our body.

The first time I got pregnant, it was difficult to accept. Pregnancy was an anxious mental struggle. I felt it as the breakdown of an equilibrium already precarious in itself, as a revelation of the animal nature behind the fragile mask of the human. For nine months I was on a seesaw of joy and horror. The birth was terrible, it was wonderful. Taking care of a newborn, by myself, without help, without money, exhausted me; I hardly slept. I wanted to write and there was never time. Or if there was some, I would concentrate for a few

27

minutes and then fall asleep fretfully. Until slowly everything began to seem to me marvellous. Today I think that nothing is comparable to the joy, the pleasure, of bringing another living creature into the world.

Of course, it took a lot of time away from my passion for writing. As a girl I'd imagined myself without children, entirely absorbed by my own yearnings. I admired women who were childless by choice, and I still understand the rejection of maternity. What I can no longer tolerate is the lack of understanding for women who do everything possible to get pregnant. In the past I had an ironic attitude, I thought: if you want children so much, adopt them. Today I think that the most extraordinary thing in my life was to conceive and give birth.

Men have always been jealous of that experience which is ours alone, and often dreamed—in myths, in certain rites—of forms of male pregnancy. Not only that: they immediately appropriated conception and birth metaphorically. They conceive ideas, give birth to works. And they have convinced us that since we already had the animal prerogative of maternity, the profoundly human prerogative of giving form to the world through sublime works was theirs alone.

But now we are demonstrating that we, too, are capable of metaphoric births, shadows are looming over maternity that seem to me threatening. A uterus can be bought. And among the countless prosthetic devices that will advance the connotations of the human there is one, the artificial uterus, that will free us from the annoyances of pregnancy.

I believe that in this case we should absolutely not be freed. Children are our body's great, marvellous prostheses, and we will not give them literally to anyone, not to mad fathers, not to the country, not even to those machines that promise an inhumanly perfect humanity.

# Odious Women

*17 March 2018*

On principle, I refuse to speak badly of another woman, even if she has offended me intolerably. It's a position that I feel obliged to take precisely because I'm well aware of the situation of women: it's mine, I observe it in others, and I know that there is no woman who does not make an enormous, exasperating effort to get to the end of the day. Poor or affluent, ignorant or educated, beautiful or ugly, famous or unknown, married or single, working or unemployed, with children or without, rebellious or obedient, we are all deeply marked by a way of being in the world that, even when we claim it as ours, is poisoned at the root by millennia of male domination.

Women live amid permanent contradictions and unsustainable labours. Everything, really everything, has been codified in terms of male needs—even our underwear, sexual practices, maternity. We have to be women according to roles and modalities that make men happy, but we also have to confront men, compete in public places, making them more and better than they are, and being careful not to offend them.

A young woman I'm very fond of said to me: it's always a problem with men, I've had to learn not to overdo. She meant that she had trained herself not to be too beautiful, too intelligent, too considerate, too independent, too generous, too aggressive, too nice. The "too" of a woman produces violent male reactions and, in addition, the enmity of other women, who every day are obliged to fight among themselves for the crumbs left by men. The "too" of men produces general admiration and positions of power.

The consequence is that not only is female power suffocated but also, for the sake of peace and quiet, we suffocate ourselves. Even today, after a century of feminism, we can't fully be ourselves, don't belong to ourselves. Our defects, our cruelties, our crimes, our virtues, our pleasure, our very language are obediently inscribed in the hierarchies of the male, are punished or praised according to codes that don't really belong to us and therefore wear us out. It's a condition that makes it easy to become odious to others and to ourselves. To demonstrate what we are with an effort at autonomy requires that we maintain a ruthless vigilance over ourselves.

So I feel close to all women, and, sometimes for one reason, sometimes for another, I recognise myself in the best as well as in the worst. Is it possible, people say to me at times, that you don't know even one bitch? I know some, of course: literature is full of them and so is everyday life. But, all things considered, I'm on their side.

# Daughters

*24 March 2018*

I very much like recognising myself in my daughters and, at the same time, feeling that they do their utmost to be different from me. Even when this attitude makes me angry, it seems positive. Not a day goes by when they don't tell me, more or less subtly, that I belong to the past. Not a day goes by when they don't point out that what I say is banal and out of touch with the present, which is their area of expertise. Not a day goes by when they don't find a way to pit their intelligence against mine, and the aim is always the same: to let me know that I should keep quiet. Not to mention that whenever I have trouble with the computer or some other electronic device, they intervene to remind me that I am of the era of the fountain pen and the pay phone.

I look at them and, sometimes with satisfaction, sometimes with alarm, see myself in their bodies, in their tone of voice. Bits of me appear for a few seconds, and I barely have time to recognise them, as when, in a page you've just written, you see flashes of the literary tradition behind you. They naturally don't notice, and that's good. I hope they have as much time as possible to declare themselves miraculously new and set about teaching me a thing or two. I, too, felt different from my mother and pushed out her generation to make room for mine. The cruelty of the latest arrivals, when they feel they're the first to come into the world, is necessary.

I greatly fear the generations who don't proudly leave their parents behind. But I'm also frightened by those who, at twenty, leave their parents behind to embrace the mores of grandparents and great-grandparents. I don't understand the young people who would replace the world of today with a golden age when everyone knew their place, that is, in an order based on sexist and racist hierarchies. Sometimes, especially when they declare themselves fascists, they don't even seem like young people, and I tend to treat them even more harshly than the old people who inspired them. Dreaming of a return to the past is a denial of youth, and it grieves me to discover that young women, too, dream those dreams.

I love young people who fight to give their time a new form and demand a better life for the entire human race. I hope my daughters stay that way for a long time. Then—it's in the natural order of things—as they get older they'll find me within themselves, discovering physical details, flashes of personality, thoughts, and will learn to welcome me, make room for me. As happened with my mother and me, they'll discover that, even admitting they're partly me, they'll continue to be themselves. In fact they'll be themselves more fully, with greater autonomy.

# The Exclamation Point                    *31 March 2018*

I try never to raise my voice. Enthusiasm, anger, even pain I try to express with restraint, tending towards self-mockery. And I admire those who maintain a calm demeanour during an argument, who try to give cautious hints that we should lower our voices, who reply to frantic questions—"Is it true it really happened like that? Is it true?"—simply with a yes or no, without exclamation marks.

Mainly, this is because I'm afraid of excesses—mine and others'. Sometimes people make fun of me. They say: "You want a world without outbursts of joy, suffering, anger, hatred?" Yes, I want precisely that, I answer. I would like it if, on the entire planet, there were no longer any reason to shout, especially with pain. I like low tones, polite enthusiasm, courteous complaints.

But as the world isn't going in that direction, I make an effort, at least in the artificial universe that is delineated by writing, never to exaggerate with an exclamation mark. Of all the punctuation marks, it's the one I like the least. It suggests a commander's staff, a pretentious obelisk, a phallic display. An exclamation should be easily understood by reading; there's no need to insist with that mark at the end as well. But I have to say that it's not simple these days.

Writers are lavish with exclamation marks. In text messages, in WhatsApp chats, in emails, I've counted up to five in a row. How much exclaiming the phony innovators of political communication engage in, the blowhards in power, young and old, who tweet nonstop every day. Sometimes I think that exclamation marks are a sign not of emotional exuberance but of aridity, of a lack of trust in written communication. I'm careful not to resort to exclamation marks in my books, but I've discovered in some of the translations an unexpected profusion of them, as if the translator had found my page sentimentally bare and devoted himself to the task of reforestation.

It's likely that my sentences sound detached; I don't rule that out. And it's likely that, where the tone for some reason is impassioned, the reader feels happier if he gets to the end of a sentence and finds the signal that authorises him to be impassioned. But I still think that "I hate you" has a power, an emotional honesty, that "I hate you!!!" does not.

At least in writing we should avoid acting like the fanatical world leaders who threaten, bargain, make deals, and then exult when they win, fortifying their speeches with the profile of a nuclear missile at the end of every wretched sentence.

# The Only True Name                    *7 April 2018*

Among the paintings in the Pio Monte della Misericordia, in
Naples—the same splendid space that houses the famous Caravaggio
devoted to the seven acts of mercy—there is a work that fascinates
me and that I go and see whenever I can. It's the figure of a nun with
hands joined, eyes closed and an ecstatic expression. The cartouche
on the right says it's *Our Lady of Solitude* a 17th-century work by an
unknown artist.

Ever since adolescence, I've liked the term "unknown." It means
that all I can know of the person who made this painting is the work
I have before my eyes. I find it a great opportunity. I can devote myself to the pure result of a creative gesture, without worrying about
a big or small name. Before me is simply the composition of a human
being who summoned his inventive energy and, rejecting countless
other possible ways of using his time, fought with the raw material
of colours to place on this surface—from within a tradition he had

behind him, and with all the ability he was capable of, forgetting even himself—his personal figure of a woman praying.

The more I look at the nun, the better I know the unknown artist of the 17th century. Not through biographical facts, not through his life story, but through his expressive strategies. In them I find inscribed in full another story—his story as an artist, which is a story of aesthetic choices, of compositional intelligence, of the grammar and syntax of an image, of feelings given shape. In the work of art, biography and autobiography have a truth completely different from that which we attribute to a CV or an income tax return. In that space there is, there has to be, a freedom of invention that allows one to violate all the agreements about truth in everyday life. To be clear: the artist of *Our Lady of Solitude* is unknown to me only on the historical-biographical level. He is very well known to me, on the other hand, in the exercise of his function as an author—so well known that I could give to that function, for convenience, a name, for example, a female name.

It would not be a pseudonym, that is, a false name; it would be the only true name used to identify her imaginative power, her ability. Every other label would be problematic, would bring into the work precisely that which has been kept out of it, so that it would stay afloat in the great river of forms. Naturally the game could also be extended to artists whom, wrongly, we don't consider "Unknown." If I had to give to the creative act of Seven Acts Of Mercy the name Caravaggio, and to the biographically determined person, the name Michelangelo Merisi, I would choose to spend the greater part of my time with Caravaggio, and not with Merisi. Merisi would blur my vision.

# The Male Story of Sex                    *14 April 2018*

Stories about heterosexual relationships interest me when they stage a violation, large or small, which doesn't conform to canonical representations. Stories with no beautiful women, for example, but ordinary ones. Or beautiful women who later reveal a physical defect. Or a handsome man hopelessly in love with a very ugly woman. When I find stories of this type in books or at the cinema or on television, I think they should be treasured, because they are small doorways through which we can glimpse different ways of narrating sex.

I'll try to explain. Tradition as a rule reinforces men's desire for the body of the woman. We're flattered, as women readers (but I would say as consumers of all the arts, including movie and television stories), with the male adoration of every part of our body. From love poems to porn, we have been represented as the most longed-for object of their passions. And convention wants our body to adhere to the model that, at a specific historical moment, is considered attractive. However one puts it, the adequacy of our body is central for the love scene to function—that is, for it to inspire the wish to receive love, to give love.

For some time now, things have seemed different, precisely as a result of the sudden increase in the number of women who write, who direct films—who try to give a form to our relations with men. It seems, however, that we still haven't been able to avoid the canon fixed by men but, despite our best intentions, have simply inserted ourselves, reinforcing it.

Female characters, especially in television, are more active, more eager, more demanding, more imaginative. Female desire explodes immediately: sometimes it's the woman who makes the first move. Yet there's little to be done: I have the impression that even today, even without wanting to, we fold and adapt to the male story of sex. If our grandmothers recognised themselves in the passive giving in to a man's desire (on the understanding that orgasms were rare, if not nonexistent), our daughters recognise themselves in the most unrestrained erotic activism—on the understanding that all that frenzy is the forced, at times painful, adaptation to behaviour that creates pleasure for men.

In this sense, stories, whether male or female, that trip up the traditional erotic narrative seem more innovative today—as opposed to those which expand the female role, making it more active than in the past. Maybe the first step in a real break with the past should be—in the era of the web and YouPorn—a female story that, while its subject is sex, isn't aphrodisiac. It's possible that our true erotic self, to begin to express itself, has need of this beginning.

# Trembling

*21 April 2018*

When it comes to religion, I recognise myself in the three Marys, who, when they go to the grave and learn from an angel that Jesus has come back to life from the dead, begin trembling, beside themselves with fear. My religious experience stopped there.

It happened when I was around sixteen. I read the gospels one after another, and the entire life of Jesus seemed terrible to me. The resurrection itself I found terrifying: not a comforting conclusion. I hope I'll have an opportunity to recount that adolescent experience of reading in detail. Here I will say only that the story of the gospels seemed to demonstrate at every step that human nature, beyond some arrogant declarations of its centrality, was depraved, devoted to either crucifying its own kind and all other living beings, or getting crucified.

But more important is the fact that even the superhuman didn't convince me—in fact, it scared me. God didn't make a good impression on my almost childlike sensibility (sixteen wasn't old enough to argue about theology). When he abandoned his son to the cross, he behaved exactly like the vile father the evangelists Luke and Matthew describe, who when his child asks for bread gives him stones, snakes, scorpions. And the resurrection? Was it really fair compensation for the extremely painful loss of earthly life, or only a horrific magic trick that didn't settle things on earth—and maybe not even the confusion of those in heaven?

Of my brief adolescent advance toward religion there remains only the fear that the three Marys express in the gospel of Mark: their trembling. I'm frightened by what the most extraordinary of Italian poets, Giacomo Leopardi, calls "the night sky full of worlds." I'm also frightened by the conceited small-mindedness of human beings when they consider themselves elect creatures. I have no liking for the throne we have assigned ourselves by declaring that we are beloved children of God and lords of the universe.

The pride that derives from that distresses me—that, although we are animals among animals, we believe we have the right to enslave the rest of the living world. This makes us dangerous, and at the same time ridiculous. However much we empower ourselves with increasingly sophisticated technology, we remain comic creatures, like the cat that a child dresses as if it were her doll. It's urgent that we learn to confront the truth of ourselves, before we're destroyed by our obstinate determination to become immortal. The animal man has to be self-critical. The future that interests me is a future of absolute openness to the other, to any living being, to everything endowed with the breath of life.

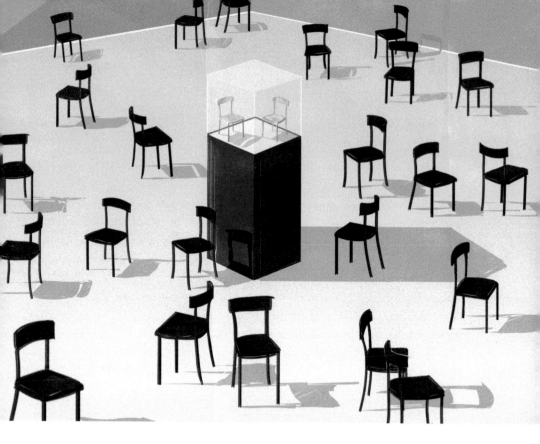

## Women Friends and Acquaintances    *28 April 2018*

I've occasionally been told by women I know that I'm a good friend. I'm pleased, and don't dare say that, in general, I tend not to put next to the word "friend" adjectives that refer to a hierarchy of feelings or reliability. They seem pointless to me. I would never say, for example, "she's my best friend," for I would have to deduce from it that I have friends I like less; others I don't trust so much; others with whom I feel less kinship. And if I did, it would occur to me to wonder: why do I consider myself the friend of these women? Why do I consider them my friends?

The word "friend," in the presence of hierarchies of this type, isn't apt. Maybe we should acknowledge that a bad friend, an unreliable friend, isn't a friend. Maybe, to be clear, even if it's painful, we should learn to say not "a friend" but "a woman I spend time with, or have spent time with." The problem is that it comforts us to have many friends—it makes us feel popular, loved, less alone. We therefore prefer to describe as "friends" women with whom we have little or nothing in common, but with whom, if necessary, we fill a void: we spend an afternoon in a cafe, we drink a glass of wine, talking about nothing in particular. Never mind if later, at the first opportunity, we call them gossips, snakes, sour, touchy.

The fact is that a woman friend is as rare as a true love. The Italian word for "friendship," *amicizia*, has the same root as the verb "to love," *amare*, and a relationship between friends has the richness, the complexity, the contradictions, the inconsistencies of love. I can say, without fear of exaggeration, that love for a woman friend has always seemed of a substance very similar to my love for the most important man in my life. Where is the difference? Sex. And it's not a small difference. Friendship isn't constantly put at risk by sexual practices, by how much danger there is in the mixture of lofty emotions and the pressure of bodies to give and be given pleasure.

It's true that today, from what I can see, sexual friendship is increasingly widespread (in Italian, I've sometimes heard the lighthearted neologism *trombamico*, or "friend with benefits"). But it's a game that seeks to keep at bay both the pervasive power of love and the rite of pure sex. We've known each other for a while, we trust each other more than strangers, we go to a bar, a restaurant, the movies, have sex.

But I still wouldn't say that it's sex between friends. Just as great loves are rare, and lovers, on the other hand, numerous, so great friends are rare; meanwhile, acquaintances with whom we may, from time to time, end up in bed are numerous.

# Digging

*5 May 2018*

There's nothing I wouldn't write about. In fact, as soon as I realize that something has flashed through my mind that I would never put in writing, I insist on doing so. Some say that you have to be vigilant, that writers shouldn't necessarily put everything into words. And part of me is absolutely in agreement. I like writing that adopts a sort of aesthetics of reticence, writing that suggests, writing that alludes.

Reticence is right and good, and certainly effective when what we are silent about is too well known to us and to our readers. It is the application of the old formula: "I leave the rest to your imagination." And the skill of the writer is best displayed when what she suggests is much more than what she says.

But I have to say that I write with greater dedication when I start digging into common, I would almost say trite, situations and feelings, and insist on expressing everything that—out of habit, to keep the peace—we tend to be silent about. I'm not interested in writing something new. I'm interested in the ordinary or, rather, what we have forced inside the uniform of the ordinary. I'm interested in digging into that and causing confusion, pushing myself to go beyond appearances. In doing so, I sometimes make myself set aside discipline and taste, because those, too, seem like blinkers. Restraint is all wrong if the task of the writing is to sweep away the resistance of the ordinary and look for words that will pull out at least a little of the extraordinary that is concealed in it. What is not suitable to say should, within the limits of the possible, be said.

I know this means that I end up writing stories that may irritate people, and in the past I was sorry about it. I like the stories that I decide to publish; I'm fond of the characters I've developed, and it makes me sad to hear someone say: "You should have stopped, but no, you continue, you go even deeper—enough." I'm talking about someone warning me that the protagonist of a story should be nice, shouldn't have terrible feelings, shouldn't do unpleasant things.

Once, a book of mine, translated and ready to be printed, wasn't even published, because—it was said—it might have a bad influence on mothers. Maybe so. We never really know what effect the stories we write have. And if we as writers make a mistake, readers have the right to punish us—by not reading our works.

But I still think that those who are more or less arbitrarily given the job of telling stories shouldn't be concerned about the serenity of individual readers; rather, they should construct fictions that help seek the truth of the human condition.

## Writing That Urges
*12 May 2018*

If you feel the need to write, you absolutely should write. Don't trust those who say: I'm telling you for your own good, don't waste time on that. The art of discouraging with kind words is among the most widely practised. Nor should you believe those who say: you're young, you lack experience, wait. We shouldn't put off writing until we've lived enough, read sufficiently, have a desk of our own in a room of our own with a garden overlooking the sea, have been through intense experiences, lived in a stimulating city, retreated to a mountain hut, have had children, have travelled extensively.

Publishing, yes: that can certainly be put off; in fact, one can decide not to publish at all. But writing should in no case be postponed to an "after." When writing is our way of being in the world, it continuously asserts itself over the countless other aspects of life: love, study, a job. It insists even when there's no paper and pen or anything, because we're worshippers of the written word and our minds dictate sentences even in the absence of tools with which to set them down. Writing, in short, is always there, urgent, and distances even the people we love, even our children who ask us to play.

The sense of guilt arrives afterwards, when we're done. If it arises before that, if we can't repress it—if, in other words, the responsibilities of affection prevail—well, maybe that's a sign that writing doesn't have sufficient power, that our vocation is fragile and that, fortunately (yes, fortunately), on the human plane we are better than artists, most of whom are so full of themselves, so egocentric.

But be careful: we have to refrain from taking our barren, proud, cruel creative deliriums for a mark of quality. The yearning to give written form to the world isn't a guarantee of good literature. Writing, even when we have a strong vocation, doesn't necessarily produce memorable work.

Oh, one can be successful, of course, transforming the fury of writing into a lucrative job. But one can never contain writing within a professional framework, complete with résumé, salary, bonuses. Success and the bit of prestige that comes with it prove nothing, especially if one's literary ambitions are high. We remain dissatisfied and, successful or not, the writing will continue to remind us that it's a tool with which one can extract much more than we have been able to. The exercise lasts obsessively, desperately, all our lives. And if others say to us, it's enough now, you've given all you could give, we don't trust that, we shouldn't trust it. Until our last breath, we'll torment ourselves with the suspicion that, just at the moment when we seem to have won, we have lost.

# Addictions

The only dependency I'm familiar with is tobacco: I started smoking when I was twelve. I was curious about taking other drugs, but not tempted. I wanted to write, and it didn't seem that doing so under the influence of alcohol or other narcotics could help: I was afraid of losing myself. Of course, quite a number of writers have obtained great results thanks to whisky or other substances, and my fear of letting go depressed me. What sort of writer could I be, if I didn't use substances that would disrupt me?

But in fact I already had my stimulant: tobacco combined with a lot of coffee. How much caffeine, how much nicotine I've absorbed over time. I stopped drinking coffee, but for decades there was nothing in my existence that wasn't accompanied by a cigarette. Pure joy for me was writing while smoking, smoking while writing. I knew it was a deceptive joy, I knew I should stop, I knew I was hurting myself and others. And at regular intervals I'd try to break out of that bondage; I'd proclaim it from the rooftops. But then I'd start up again, in secret—a clandestine passion that has more power than most, precisely because it's clandestine.

Meet strangers and not smoke? Terrible. Read and not smoke? Terrible. Write and not smoke? Terrible. Finally, for many reasons, I stopped, but it was painful. Not having a cigarette between my fingers made me anxious. I would refuse to see people I admired, whom I was fond of, whose respect and friendship I valued. I was convinced that I would do something wrong, say something rude, that nothing intelligent would come to mind, and that those people I admired would no longer respect me. In other words, I felt more inadequate than usual; I was afraid of finding out that I was much worse than I had imagined.

I discovered that I couldn't let go of cigarettes, because I was afraid of seeing the world in all its sharp-edged clarity. Cigarettes, alcohol, cocaine are to varying degrees dark glasses, and give us the impression that we can more readily tolerate the collision with life, more comfortably savour it.

But is that true? That what enslaves us empowers us? For months I believed that, without lighting a cigarette, I would be unable to write even half a line, that writing, the thing I most cared about, would be barred to me for ever. Sometimes even today, when I haven't smoked for many years, I feel convinced of that and am on the point of giving in. I've saved myself only because a very weak part of me murmurs that it's nonsense, that, really, soothing myself with forty cigarettes a day for so long kept me from writing as I should have.

# Insomnia

26 May 2018

Long ago, I used to read and write as I waited for the moment of sleep. Soon I had to stop. Reading led me to a state of overexcitement: usually, one reads a few pages to fall asleep more easily, but the more I read, the more sleep passed me by. And it wasn't a question of the quality of the books. Mediocre books, great books, novels, essays: sleep eluded me. Reading brought on a desire to write, and writing brought on a desire to read. The night passed without me closing my eyes and the next day was wasted. I was in a daze, I had a headache, I couldn't do anything.

It took me a long time to resign myself to the idea that, after eight o'clock at night, I shouldn't open a book, and I shouldn't write. It seemed a serious limitation, but it was necessary—not sleeping took away the desire to live. So I gave in, and for a while things improved. But during periods when I was writing for almost the whole day, my insomnia returned, and in a way that frightened me. I was sleeping but had the impression that I was still writing, words and words.

A doctor once told me that, even for reading and writing, you need a certain kind of body, and mine wasn't the right kind: it couldn't sustain the effort. So, having completely stopped reading and writing, I systematically exhausted myself with everyday things.

After that, I realised that writing and reading had little to do with my insomnia: I still had trouble sleeping. A fleeting half-thought was enough to open the door to an obsession: fears for my family, jealousies, dissatisfactions. In the dark, eyes wide open, I analysed in detail my behaviour and that of others; I convinced myself of disloyalties and betrayals. In other words, the late hour, when everything should grow dim and vanish, consigned me to an intolerable lucidity about myself and the people I loved, and who I thought loved me.

At around the age of thirty, I began taking sleeping pills. But, however potent they were, I managed to sleep at most three or four hours a night. At one point, I thought that surrendering completely to insomnia would help me more than the pills. So I went back to reading and writing whenever I wanted, and often didn't even go to bed. Today, I don't get much sleep at night, but I get enough in the early afternoon. If I like what I'm reading or writing, I don't close my eyes. If I don't like it, I fall into a disappointed, dissatisfied sleep. I've given in to insomnia and I get my sleep how and when I can. All in all, I'm doing fine.

# The Pleasure of Learning          *2 June 2018*

Of all the years I spent at school and university, I recall with pleasure only those of primary school. I don't mean that the rest of my education, up to my university graduation, was a waste of time: rather, I would emphasise how happy I was to discover Latin and Greek, philosophy, mathematics, chemistry, physics, geography and, especially, astronomy. School, and later university, had precisely that function: introducing me to branches of knowledge I was completely ignorant of. They said to me: there is a subject called Latin, or Greek, or philosophy, and you will study it for a certain number of years— five, three, even just one.

But it never seemed that knowing Latin or Greek had a value in itself; it meant, for example, being able to read the works of Euripides or Seneca in the language in which they were written. I considered them purely subjects for academic training; studying them was useful for getting a diploma, or for a possible job. It wasn't learning, but a continuous obedient exercise that led to a position high up in the hierarchy of cleverness.

I was usually one of the best, and yet the ideas that I memorised in order to shine have all faded. I've forgotten everything, and I'm not happy about it: how much wasted struggle. Not only do I have nothing left in my head—I have the impression that I studied very hard without learning, that I made an enormous effort without a moment of enjoyment.

My primary school years, on the other hand, have left a very clear memory of the wonder with which the hours at the desk were transformed into precise skills—reading, writing, counting—but also into numerous additional bits of information. I wouldn't today be able to describe in detail how that feeling of proud wonder took shape; there, too, memory has faded, and I'd have to invent convincing anecdotes, because I can't remember any particular thing.

But the wonder—the wonder of knowing how to read, to write, to transform signs into things, landscapes, people, feelings, voices, or, vice versa, how to reduce all reality, and every fantasy, every plan, into signs of the alphabet, into numerals—the wonder has remained vivid and lasting. Of the years that followed, I remember the hard work, the anxiety to do well, some humiliations, some nasty failures, a number of successes—but never that satisfying sense of wonder.

To my surprise, I suddenly started to learn again some time after I graduated. It no longer happens these days, but I hope that in the free time of old age, the wonder will return.

## Discontent

I have never undergone psychoanalytic therapy, but I've always been on the point of doing it. What pushed me? Often a feeling of inadequacy. More often a feeling of excess, one that made me feel as if I had drunk so much water that I was drowning in it. And then a sense of permanent discontent, always stifled by my habit of good manners. And then the tendency to distance every desire that wasn't consistent with the idea I had of myself. And finally, a faint unhappiness that wouldn't go away—like minor joint pain that one learns to live with.

What, on the other hand, made me hold back? The idea of telling an unknown person, someone with no weight in my life, everything that passed through my mind. I had no wish to. It seemed like a violence that I was agreeing to submit to—devoutly paying for it. I felt I would be giving in to blackmail. I took for granted a sort of mute speech by the prospective analyst that went like this: I have the power to help you, but if you want me to exercise that power, you have to provide for me, at a fixed time, and in exchange for money, memories, thoughts, beliefs, everything, even the lies you tell.

To sneak away from the need I felt for analysis, I used the excuse of lack of money. You can't worsen your family's financial situation to improve your own, I said to myself. And I consoled myself by thinking: there are so many people who don't have the money; your discontent is part of the discontent of an enormous slice of the human race that surely needs help more than you do.

But even when my financial situation improved, I did not go to therapy. I refused to form a relationship in which I would be in a subordinate position, forced to yield to the enormous power of someone who is silent while you ramble on, asking you questions without ever really responding to yours, concealing from you his drives – while you reveal yours in the most vulnerable way.

Today I would go to therapy without making excuses; in fact, I would give free rein to a decades-long impulse. The moment has arrived, I say to myself. I have no financial problems, and, especially, I no longer have the need to prove to myself that I will not be subject to any power, great or small. Then what holds me back? Probably I've read too much and my curiosity has diminished. Probably I think, presumptuously, that I know enough to explain myself to myself, without recourse to experts. Probably, as I grow old, my discontent has also grown old, and is as if asleep. Probably—and perhaps this is the real point—I was never truly ill. Those who are truly ill must, and do, look for help right away.

# Winners and Losers                    *16 June 2018*

I don't like the classification of human beings into winners and losers. Or maybe I don't understand it. I think of the symbols that identify a winner. Money, above all—that is to say, the possibility of acquiring expensive objects, and a taste for displaying them as proof of your superiority. Or the exercise of power, demonstrating by very subtle means that you are high up in the hierarchy. Or the sort of aristocracy that derives from media fame, a blue blood of celebrity ensuring that you don't have to earn people's attention every time—you're recognised enthusiastically, at first sight. Or the permanent mise-en-scène of happiness: someone who has a lot of money exercises power, enjoys the status of a VIP, and therefore must be happy.

Except that all these symbols of the winner's position soon reveal themselves to be less than genuine and, above all, precarious. Money, power, fame, glory, happiness—all are quick to show cracks. And every time this image of the winner collapses, and the appearance of victory turns to failure, the idea of the loser collapses, too; that category of people who have no expensive possessions, no power, no fame, only a sense of unhappiness resulting from their impression of having failed.

Maybe the true spectre behind this classification into winners and losers is precisely that, the fear of failure. It was the thing that as a girl I feared most. Failing in school; failing to get a job; failing any test, be it athletics or maths. I put an exhausting amount of effort into everything that had even the appearance of a competition, because I sensed that one failure leads to another, and that that's where the list of the good and the bad originates. When you end up on the list of the bad, it becomes difficult to cross over on to the list of the good.

It took me a long time to understand that those classifications are as cruel as they are arbitrary. They pretend that neither socioeconomic inequalities nor sexual and racial discrimination exist, nor the extremely culpable waste of intelligence that results. We draw up lists of the good and the bad as if the many privileges deriving from chance aren't there: your place of birth, your family, the inequality of opportunities.

Even today, in this so-called advanced part of the world, the conditions at the point of starting out are too unjust to think of as a competition in which the odds are not stacked. If I could, I would eliminate concepts such as failing, winning and losing, which no longer have any basis. If it were really necessary, I would confine myself to a competition like the caucus race that Alice encounters in Wonderland. Nobody loses, everybody wins and there is no failure.

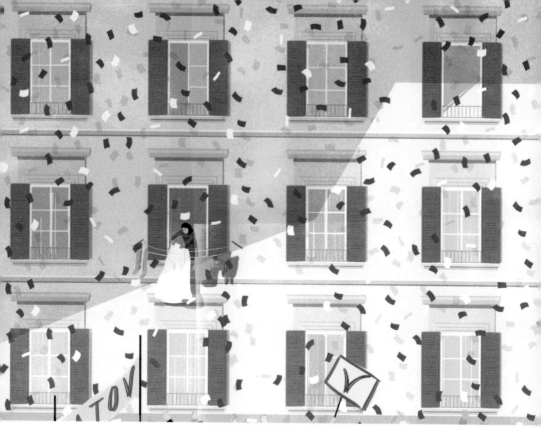

# Bad Feelings

*22 June 2018*

I've never been politically active. I've never organized marches or demonstrations, or helped organize them. I've confined myself to taking part in initiatives that seemed urgent, and necessary for the common good. There have been times when I was truly alarmed, and feared for the fate of democracy in my country. But more often I've thought our worries have been deliberately exaggerated.

I've never shared the apprehension about the political rise of the Five Star Movement, and find the term "populism"—today applied to all political forces, old and new—to be useless. The Five Star Movement has seemed an important receptacle for the mass discontent generated by the inadequate, often disastrous way—on right and left, in Italy and across Europe—governments have dealt with the economic crisis and epochal changes we are living through.

I've never voted for Five Star: its muddled, sometimes naive, sometimes banal language is alien to me. But I still think it's an extremely serious mistake to portray the movement as a danger to Italian democracy and, more generally, to Europe. The war against Five Star has prevented us from seeing that the danger is elsewhere. I'm referring to Matteo Salvini's League, a political force that is much better organized, and deceptively tamed by years of governing with Berlusconi. I have no fondness for Salvini. I dislike what he represents, just as I dislike what those to whom he gives a lot of credit represent on this planet: Putin, Trump and, in their wake, Marine Le Pen, Viktor Orbán and others.

Salvini, federal secretary of the League—the most significant part of our new government—is in line with the worst of the Italian political traditions. Widely underestimated, used by television producers to enliven debates and generate publicity, he has become increasingly persuasive, giving the appearance of a good-natured common man who thoroughly understands the problems of the common people and at the right moment bangs his xenophobic and racist fists on the table.

Sometimes I imagine, anxiously, that the consensus around the bad feelings Salvini embodies (and stimulates) may spread beyond his intentions and slide into the mass brutality that in times of crisis is always lying in wait, welding divergent motives: those of profit, and broad sectors of society demoralized by their economic precariousness and fear of the future.

Five Star wanted to govern to rescue the country from inefficiency. But today they seem to be sitting on the benches of parliament—prime minister Giuseppe Conte at their head—in order to assume all the blame that normally goes to the politicians in power. Their first accuser, in due course, will be Salvini.

# Ellipses

*30 June 2018*

Some cautious notes on ellipses. They are pleasing. They're like stepping stones, the sort that stick out of the water and are a risky pleasure to jump on when you want to cross a stream without getting wet. Today, especially in emails and texts, they have such power of suggestion that we distribute them by the handful. The canonical three dots are no longer enough; there are four, five, even six. "I'm here... I'm in anguish.... I wonder where you are..... I'm thinking of you...... I would like to see you again but......."

They're very communicative and indicate many things: anxiety, embarrassment, timidity, uncertainty, the mischief of saying and not saying, a moment when we were about to exaggerate and then let it go, or even just a pause.

I used to use them freely; now I don't use them at all. And yet I like them: in other people's writing they don't bother me, even if instead of three dots I find ten in a row. But at a certain point, my eyes started to fly over those dots, moving on to grab hold of the words as quickly as possible. And in my own writing I began to feel they were flirtatious, like someone batting her eyelashes, mouth slightly open in feigned wonder. Too many graceful winking suspensions, in short.

I stopped using them definitively when, as a result of personal experience, I became convinced that no discourse, once begun, should ever be suspended. I'm talking about oral communication: if you take on the responsibility of starting a sentence, you should bring it to an end—even if you're being shouted at, even if you're being insulted, and you regret that you started to speak, and you flounder, lose confidence, the words no longer come to you.

My decision didn't have anything to do with writing, and maybe not even with ellipses; it had to do with the very idea of suspension. Sometimes we're silent to keep the peace, sometimes out of self-interest, knowing we shouldn't speak or everything will be ruined. But more often we're silent out of fear, out of complicity. Silence can be criticised, but it has the virtue of being a clear choice. It's when we decide to break it, to speak, that we have to get to the end without slipping away, without the convenience of ellipses.

An old inclination for the fade-out has changed over the years into an aversion to prevaricating, to the secretive signal. If you have to speak, then speak, I say to myself, and get to the end. Even when dialogue imposes an ellipsis—in novels, they get out of hand—I do everything to avoid it. If I can't, I prefer to reduce them from three to one, an abrupt interruption—so instead of "I'd like to see you again but..." I prefer "I'd like to see you again but." You have to pay the price in a cut-off sentence, note its ugliness, and rectify it by learning to get, at least when it comes to words, to the point.

11A ▶                          12                              1

# Works of Art

*7 July 2018*

In the course of my life, I have had intense emotional relationships with the screen versions of many actors and actresses, on both the big and small screen. My latest attachment has been to the shadow that, for the sake of convenience, I will call Daniel Day-Lewis. Is it a physical attraction? Perhaps. Let's say he certainly corresponds to a type of man I like: lean, slightly receding hairline, a long face where the features are not annoyingly symmetrical.

This is not a long-winded way of describing what excites me about this particular male body; rather, I'm being deliberately generic. The reason is, Daniel Day-Lewis interests me as much as any other lean man with a slightly receding hairline and features that are not annoyingly symmetrical. Let's say I have no curiosity about what he is really like, and that if I happened to meet him on the street I probably wouldn't even recognise him. I love him only in his films. I love him for the way the light on the set calculatedly strikes him, for the way he is photographed, for the power of the plot his body moves through, for the intelligence of the remarks that someone else wrote and he speaks, for the imagination with which a director has directed him, for the skill of the makeup artist, for the costumes he wears, and so on.

I long ago stopped thinking of stars as human beings who truly exist. I know that at the origin of the love that films, or story factories, inspire in us there is not a physical person but a collection of specialties. When I love Daniel Day-Lewis, I love the novelists from whose books his films are adapted, the screenwriters who have composed the dialogue, and the film directors, the directors of photography, the lighting and sound technicians, the set designers, the acting coaches – in other words, all those who have helped to make his real body—with its mimetic ability, its gait, way of gesticulating, its photogenic quality—into a body particularly suited to becoming a movie or television icon.

Daniel Day-Lewis (like any star, or perhaps any creative person) is, in short, not a man but a work of art. His name is a sort of title by which I refer to a valuable body of work—that is to say, the sum of all the characters he has so brilliantly portrayed, all the plots into which he has been inserted. In other words, he is a marvellous product of the imagination, a phantom moulded with words and images and technical equipment and professional skill.

And he'd be that, if you think about it, even if I had the pleasure of knowing him and spending time with him. If he should suddenly be transformed into a flesh-and-blood person, poor him, poor me. Reality can't stay inside the elegant moulds of art; it always spills over, indecorously.

## The Deluge of News                    *14 July 2018*

I don't feel desperate to be informed about everything that happens in the world. As a girl, I merely glanced at the newspaper headlines and occasionally watched the TV news.

But a growing interest in politics, which erupted when I was around twenty, inspired me to amass information. It seemed to me that until then I'd lived in a state of distraction, and I was afraid I'd go through life without even being aware of the disasters, the horrors around me. I feared I would become a superficial person, unconsciously complicit. So I forced myself to read the newspapers, and then since that didn't seem sufficient, moved on to books of contemporary history, sociology, philosophy. There was a period when, against my nature, I even stopped reading novels: it seemed like time stolen from the need to live in my own era with eyes wide open.

But I didn't make great progress: I always felt as if I'd entered a theatre where the movie had already started and I was struggling to get oriented. Where was the good, where was the evil? Who was the just, who the unjust? Who was interpreting facts, and who twisting them to create propaganda?

This struggle isn't over. In fact, it seems to me more difficult today than in the past to try to understand how the world is going, in order not to have to discover, in the end, that in our distraction we have been complicit with the dregs of the human race. The uninterrupted rain of news doesn't help, books don't help, the constantly new sociological terms that brilliantly simplify reality don't help. Rather, I have the impression that today's network of information, in both its print and digital manifestations, forces citizens into a sort of chaos, a condition in which the more informed you are, the more confused you are. For me, the problem is not, therefore, to stay well informed but to track within the mass of pointlessly amplified news that which will help me to distinguish, over time, the true and the false, the best and the worst: this is an extremely difficult task.

I've always had great admiration for those who, in the chaos that generally characterises the present, sensed from the start the enormous dangers of Nazi-fascism and courageously denounced it. But do we still have the capacity to be as far-seeing? Do the conditions exist today for the long view?

Sometimes I think I understand why we women increasingly read novels. Novels, when they work, use lies to tell the truth. The information marketplace, battling for an audience, tends, more and more, to transform intolerable truths into novelistic, riveting, enjoyable lies.

## Literary Novelty

There was a phase—fortunately long past—when I was convinced that a story either had to be absolutely new, comparable to nothing but itself, or it must be discarded. This was a very presumptuous and at the same time naive attitude. It assumed that I was endowed with extraordinary gifts, and that if these gifts were not manifested in works of utter, precious uniqueness, I would have to conclude either that I was betraying myself, out of laziness or sloppiness, or that my assumption was completely unfounded. In other words, what I wrote had to be better than, and at the same time completely different from, the books that I loved and that had inspired my yearning to tell stories.

Today, I don't have much faith in those who say, "Here is a truly new book." What is truly new in literature is only our uniquely individual way of using the storehouse of the world's literature. We are immersed in what has preceded us. I don't mean the schoolbooks that chronologically order authors, their lives and works, from the beginning to now, nor do I mean the meticulous list of what we have read, starting from the age of seven. There is no before of which we are the after. All literature, great or small, is in that sense contemporary: it crowds around us as we write; it's the air we breathe.

Consequently, our pages are never "new" in the sense that the culture industry gives the adjective. No author produces texts without debts. There are no works that make a clean break with the past, works that exclude it—no truly watershed works. Literary novelty— if one wants to insist on the concept—exists in the way each individual inhabits the magma of forms he is immersed in. Thus "to be oneself" is an arduous task—perhaps impossible.

Being oneself does not mean being "new." I'm surprised by those who provocatively flaunt their own "novelty," who consider themselves unique, who don't want to admit influences. It's a spectacular exhibition of arrogance, for the use of the media; or a manifestation of the terror of not having any individuality—as if it could be proved only by denying the literary material that has established and establishes us. Not even Homer was ever "new."

The individual author takes shape every time, thanks to the effort of deconstructing the literary tradition and putting it back together in startling forms. And that's not at all a small thing.

# Lies

As a child, I was a big liar; I told all kinds of lies. I lied in order to seem better than I was. I lied to boast about things I would like to have done, but hadn't. I often got into real trouble, because I was consistent with my lies, confessing sins that I had committed only in a lie. I told anguished lies—painful to remember—improvised in a hurry to avoid some act of violence, usually on the part of boys.

But the lies that I liked best—and I told quite a number of them—served absolutely no purpose. I put a lot into them and did all I could to make them seem like things that had really happened. They seemed so true that even I, as I was speaking, had the impression they weren't lies. Or maybe it's the opposite: I would tell lies without considering them lies, so they gave a stronger appearance of truth.

That kind of lie belongs to the happy side of my childhood. I was very successful with my peers, who were beguiled by my stories; they believed me and would have listened to me for ever. But then, sometimes, someone would say: it's too good, it can't really have happened. And then I was a little ashamed; I began to swear to the truth of the story, and at the same time I was sorry. I became anxious, I felt that the game was being spoiled. What should I do? Make the lies repellent? But what pleasure would there be in telling them, if I made them boring, incoherent?

Maybe it was because of those criticisms that, around the age of twelve, I decided not to lie any more. Perhaps I simply wanted to become adult, and telling lies seemed childish. So, as I've done often in my life, overnight I imposed on myself a fierce discipline, and I stopped telling lies. To compensate, I became a good oral narrator of all kinds of events. I recounted my dreams and nightmares, making an effort to be extremely faithful. I summarised novels and films for my friends, and the summaries were very detailed. Sometimes, too, I recounted things that had really happened to me—careful, however, not to adjust them to make them flow better, or in a more engaging way.

Yet for years I felt nostalgia for the long, cogent and gratuitous lies of the child: I had the impression that they were truer than the truth. That nostalgia is probably what later led me to give a narrative style to the diaries I kept, and started me writing novels, where I could explore the possibilities of the particular type of lie that is the story.

Anyway, novels or not, the nostalgia remains. I love children who tell lies for no reason—I immediately recognise the pleasure. And I also recognise the anguish—the anguish when children lie to protect themselves—because the world is full of traps and humiliations, and the lie can sometimes give us a little respite.

# Confessing

*4 August 2018*

I have learned that bad feelings are inevitable; if we want to be honest with ourselves and others, we have to confess them. It's a matter of discipline.

How? First of all, by forcing ourselves not to disguise them as the feelings of a fearless person who holds the truth paramount. Are we tormented by that good-natured female friend whom everyone likes, while we have to struggle for a crumb of affection? Fine: we shouldn't react by telling everyone that her success is the result of some carefully orchestrated hypocrisy. Above all, we shouldn't justify our slander by saying that it is a love of the truth that drives us: that makes us as much a hypocrite as she is.

Instead, make an effort. Let's teach ourselves to think that her good nature is innate, and that to reduce it to a skilful exercise in hypocrisy is simply a sign of the envy we feel. This effort, of course, benefits no one: we remain envious, and we continue to suffer from it. Surely we felt better when we were playing the role of the outspoken person, fighting against duplicity?

So then what to do? Well, we have to make another effort: find the proper tone in which to tell our friend that her success makes us suffer, that we envy her, that we're ashamed of ourselves when, instead of admitting that she possesses qualities we don't, we go around saying she's a hypocrite. If we can do this, we will have taken two giant steps forward. First, we will have discovered that we protect the truth principally by telling the truth about ourselves. And, second, we will have gained something much more admirable than an innate good nature: the capacity for self-examination and self-control.

But what if our friend really is a hypocrite? Never mind. It's a dangerous game to play and she'll soon be discovered; she'll lose the reputation she's gained and we'll be glad. Yes, glad, and yet again we'll have to reckon with a bad feeling: the malicious pleasure of witnessing the fall of successful people, the satisfaction of recording their dismay and despair after a happy period.

How shall we proceed? Will we feel ourselves in the right, will we triumphantly tell everyone that we were among the first to guess that our friend—now no longer our friend—was a hypocrite? No: yet again, we'll make an effort to be truthful with ourselves. We'll admit that we enjoy the misfortunes of others, we'll admit that they give us some relief. From St Augustine of Hippo onwards, speaking with fierce candour, not to others but to ourselves, sometimes absolutely saves us.

# Clean Breaks

*18 August 2018*

I have never been particularly frightened of change. I've moved house a few times, but I don't remember particular discomforts, regrets, long periods of maladjustment. A lot of people hate moving; some people think it can shorten your life. But first of all, I love the word—in Italian, *trasloco*, or "across a place"—which makes me think of the momentum needed for a leap forward, a gathering of energy that propels you towards another place, where there is everything to discover and learn.

I am convinced, in other words, that change has a definite positive side. It helps us realize, for example, that we've accumulated a lot of useless things: very little is truly of use. We get attached to objects and spaces, and sometimes people; and find that without them, not only is our life not impoverished, it unexpectedly opens up to new possibilities.

When such changes are radical, my tendency, after a little hesitation, is towards euphoria. I feel the way I did when, as a child, I invented all kinds of reasons to be outside when a storm was approaching and the air was charged with electricity, and I could smell the rain arriving, feel the first drops, and wanted to get completely soaked before my mother grabbed me and pulled me inside.

That propensity, however, meant that it took me a culpably long time to feel the other side of change: suffering. I don't mean so much the discomfort of small changes, but the devastating force of big changes when they destroy old models of life and invent and impose new ones. There is, to start with, the suffering of people who are overwhelmed, who suddenly see their existence in a shambles: they rage, resist from within the shell of old habits, give up hope and, finally, collapse when they discover that the world of yesterday will not be here tomorrow. It's the suffering that accompanies a way of life in decline.

And yet I've never been drawn in—not even through literature— by regret for how wonderful life used to be. I've always felt the joy of upheaval, and maybe that's why my relatively recent discovery of the suffering inherent in change has made a deep impression. If we look beyond the joy that has greeted the many revolutions in the lives of women, we find just as much real suffering. And yet, as far as I know, the pain of those changes has hardly been described at all.

Even as a liberating act, taking off a dress that we've always worn, sometimes from the first years of life, to put on one that is more fitting, more festive, more audacious, more authoritative, can hurt somewhere. We can't tear off what once seemed to be our skin without pain; something endures and resists. Certainly the joyful sense of liberation prevails; but to be silent about the anguish, the suffering is a mistake. The anaesthetic doesn't cancel out the wound.

# Mothers

My mother was very beautiful and very clever, like all mammas, so I loved her and hated her. I began to hate her when I was around ten, maybe because I loved her so much that the idea of losing her threw me into a permanent state of anxiety, and to calm myself I had to belittle her.

Sometimes she seemed to me to be beautiful and clever just so that everyone would see me as ugly and stupid. I couldn't think any thought of my own; I had only her thoughts in my mind. I felt oppressed, tormented by her mania for order, by her outmoded tastes that suffocated mine, by her idea of just and unjust. For a long time, I felt that to stop loving her was the only way I had to love myself— even to have a myself to love.

A secret cord that can't be cut binds us to the bodies of our mothers: there is no way to detach ourselves, or at least I've never managed to. It's impossible to go back inside her; it's hard to move past her shadow.

So I quickly put many other bodies between hers and mine—bodies with which I could be the boss, quarrel, make love, appear wise or foolish—constructing a world alien to hers. I wanted her to feel uneasy if she merely looked in on it: that happened often, and she escaped in silence.

Over the years, she withdrew. She got smaller, she lost beauty and cleverness, she stopped asserting her own superiority in everything, her words no longer had weight.

For a while I felt free. Then people began to say things like, "You laugh like your mother, you're stubborn like your mother, you have your mother's hands." One morning I looked at myself in the mirror and I recognised her: she was there, in my body. And to my surprise it began to bother me less and less; slowly I discovered her in my gestures, in a particular way of showing or controlling feelings, in my voice. If it was impossible to go back inside my mother, it was very possible that she had been inside me since birth, and that she could be found inside me even when I fought to escape her—even when I thought I was free of her.

Ever since I realised that finding myself meant finding her, and accepting and loving her the way I did as a child, I have felt soothed. Sometimes reconciliation is taken to be the capacity to forget the wrongs we've suffered. And maybe it's true, but not in our relations with our mothers. I was reconciled with mine when I felt those wrongs—what seemed to me wrongs—as part of myself, essential for my development. So essential that they now appear an invention of mine, a brightly coloured exaggeration.

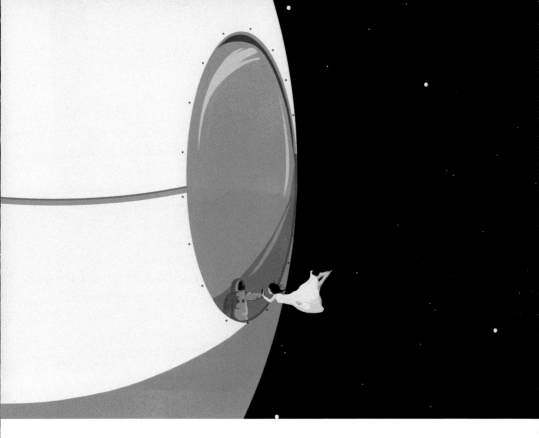

# At the Movies

A film that I watch at least once a year is Andrei Tarkovsky's *Solaris*. I've loved all of Tarkovsky's works, even the most difficult. Some I've seen in the cinema, others on television. I saw *Andrei Rublev* at the cinema, and on the big screen it was astonishing, its black and white extraordinary: I'll probably never see it again in a cinema, but I hope that young people will have the opportunity.

I also saw *Solaris* on the big screen—not Tarkovsky's best film, but the one that made the greatest impression on me. I remember that it was advertised as the Soviet answer to *2001: A Space Odyssey*— a completely misleading slogan. To see in it a cinematic contest between the US and the USSR was as silly as it was misleading. Kubrick's marvellous film, with its imaginative force, would certainly win. But it doesn't have even a hint of the desperation, of the sense of loss, that dominates *Solaris*.

The version that was shown at the time was cut, and I didn't see the uncut version until later. But in both versions, the power lies in the female character, in that memory of a woman who can't vanish into oblivion. What struck me and disoriented and frightened me—*Solaris* is still a film that seduces and at the same time scares me, more than any thriller or horror film—was the woman's atrocious deaths and implacable resurrections, her obstinate persistence, the fierce and at the same time self-destructive will not to be definitively annihilated by the beloved man even as pure memory. If I had to make a list of the most authentic female characters invented by the great male directors, I don't know if I would put the woman in *Solaris* at the top, but certainly I would place her in the first ranks—because of the blind suffering she emanates, because of her serene yet furious refusal to be eliminated.

*Solaris* is also astonishing because the book by Stanislaw Lem that inspired it, while powerful, doesn't seem to contain Tarkovsky's film. The page can stimulate a surprising visionary force when a great talent finds the necessary nourishment in it.

Many years later, the American director Steven Soderbergh gave us another *Solaris*, one that also started from Lem's text. But this time it didn't produce a memorable film. The processes that lead from words to images are mysterious. Tarkovsky read in Lem his own need and urgency; Soderbergh tried to but couldn't. Or maybe Tarkovsky's *Solaris* left no room for the birth of another great film. Written words can generate a wide variety of film versions, but a great one is so particular, so commanding, that, once made, it bars the way to any other masterpiece.

## Happy Childhoods

*8 September 2018*

I don't have much to do with children these days. Friends and relatives send me photographs and videos of their children. I save this material carefully: I like comparing the face of a newborn with what he or she has become at eight months, at two years, at three. I have no photographs of myself as a newborn; the first image goes back to when I was two. Whereas there's not a day in the life of my granddaughter that has not been entrusted to the future, thanks to her parents' mobile phones, which are always within reach.

And thanks to these photos and videos, I could describe in detail how the form of the newborn has become the form of a child. If I were to make a film out of this material, I would get an interminable but impressive documentary on the instability of our bodies from birth—the way they continually take shape and lose shape, how they explore the possibilities in an effort to understand what to become, but never find a fixed form. Not to mention crawling, learning to stand upright, the infinite attempts at language, the manipulation of objects: there is a lot you could do with this abundant crop of family images.

Naturally, only the marvels of the child are documented. Beauty triumphs, along with appeal, charm, joy, happy laughter. The videos break off as soon as the child screams, gets angry, turns ugly. Missing is the distress, tiredness, irritation, fear, tantrums. Missing are the tensions between the parents that alarm children, and heighten their uneasiness.

Occasionally, a video begins when the child has just stopped crying and, her features again relaxed, she is ready for play, even though one eye is still slightly veiled by tears. There is very little that documents the painful side of growing up, of childhood unhappiness and the effort of existing. If the mobile phones were allowed to do their work on that as well, what grim videos would we have? Taking shape and losing it would become an unpleasant spectacle, with horror-film moments.

I use the word "spectacle" deliberately, because all these materials are produced not only as a document; they also seek an audience. Parents of single children—or sometimes two children—in presenting the best of their offspring present themselves at their best as fathers and mothers, and they do it for uncles, grandparents, actual friends and virtual ones. Of course they put those bits of happiness on stage; the rest they leave in the wings. Living it is already arduous: imagine filming it.

The result, perhaps, is that my granddaughter, when she tries to locate, in this inexhaustible flow of images, her own "I," unhappy like all of us, will have trouble finding herself, will wonder: if that's me, so pretty, so lively, so capable, how did I become like this? The vast documentation will be as insufficient as my single photo of a two-year-old, which only by convention I call "Me at two." "Me" who? We'll always know too little about ourselves.

# Interviews

I am not very good at speaking, in public or private. If it's a matter of recounting facts, I manage more or less to bring them to a conclusion. But if I have to explain my reasoning, argue rigorously, I get agitated, confused—everything seems to fly out of my head. Things go badly in particular if I'm dealing with people who I think have some authority. I have everything clear in my mind to start with, and yet it's as if, after a few words, something gives way. I lose faith in what I wanted to say, the taut thread of the argument I had in mind breaks, I keep repeating: "I'm sorry, but I can't explain."

On the very rare occasions when I have had to speak in public, I spent days preparing a text. I memorised it, so as to give the impression of speaking spontaneously; but I ended up reading it line for line and, naturally, boring the audience, who prefer speakers who improvise and know how to stir the emotions, how to entertain.

I, too, admire people who have that ability, and I've made an effort to accept the fact that I don't. I feel master of myself—insofar as anyone can be master of herself—only if I write. Even interviews, in the end, become a flight from speech, an exercise in writing.

Some people reproach me for giving so few interviews, and some consider that I give too many. Almost thirty years ago, when journalists first asked to interview me, I prevaricated, then refused. In reality, although I use the word myself, I have never "given an interview." In interviews, the subject entrusts her body, her facial expressions, her eyes, gestures and, above all, her way of speaking to the writing of the interviewer—a conversation that is improvised, temperamental, disjointed. Against the face-to-face encounter, I have preferred—because of my own limitations—a written correspondence. The journalist thinks about it and writes me her questions; I think about it and write my answers.

In the past I didn't think I was capable of organising answers suitable for publication. Or they seemed too compact, often a yes or a no. A question of a few lines became an occasion for reflection, and then I wrote pages and pages.

Now I seem to have learned how, and I find these written exchanges increasingly useful—for myself, naturally. It results in writing that should be set beside the books like a fiction not very different from the literary one. I invent myself for a journalist, but the journalist—especially when she is herself a writer—invents herself for me, through her questions. And I address not only the interviewer and our eventual readers but also myself, or at least that substantial part of myself that considers using up so much time writing—being an author—senseless, and needs reasons to justify this waste of a life.

# Love Forever

The relationships of couples are an effective embodiment of the precariousness of our lives. If we meet someone we haven't seen for several months, we hesitate to say: "Tell Franco hello from me." It's better to find out first, through circumspect questioning, if the relationship with Franco is still on, or if he has been replaced by a Gianni or a Giorgio, because even the most long-term relationships can end suddenly, and no one—today more than in the past—knows the formula for ensuring a marriage will last.

A very old friend of mine, who has been married for exactly forty-eight years, to a good man, says that in fact there is a formula: you just have to love each other. The problem, she adds in an amused tone, is that loving each other for a lifetime is really arduous.

First, you have to always be attractive to each other, in bed and elsewhere, even if the body is continually changing, even if what first drew you is gone. Second, you have to appreciate not only the virtues of your partner (too easy) but also the vices, especially those that in the beginning were well hidden. Third, you have to constantly demonstrate your great respect for him, even when it's clear you've made a mistake and he doesn't deserve your respect, because he's a perfectly normal idiot. Fourth, you have to immediately look the other way when your fidelity is casually repaid with betrayal, and meanwhile hope at least to be betrayed with discretion, just as you will surely do as soon as you observe that being faithful earns you nothing but humiliation. Fifth, you have to repress the desire to break everything and leave, to persuade yourself that the children need a father, even when he's terrible, that growing old in solitude is far worse than growing old together, and that becoming adult means accepting life as it is—that is to say, repugnant. Sixth, you have to believe, finally, that loving—loving with your feet on the ground, not what you imagined as a girl—is a skilful juggling exercise, a permanent sacrifice, elegantly swallowing a bitter pill.

There, my friend says, laughing, a relationship can last a lifetime. I asked her: has your marriage lasted nearly fifty years because this is what you and your husband did? She answered, annoyed: what do you mean, we've been fortunate, we have a strong bond, we love each other deeply. Certainly there are couples who are both happy and stable, and her marriage is of that type—not to be discussed.

So I didn't discuss it any more. We went back to talking with amusement about couples, betrayals, furtive sex. People always do this, even when we know we're talking about tragedies equal to a nuclear war. The light smile is useful. It's an escape route when, for a few seconds, in the stories of others, we get a painful glimpse of our own.

# No Reason                                    *29 September 2018*

I've had enemies and still do. I'm sorry about it, but that's how it is. How enmity begins I don't know; every generalisation seems arbitrary. I have a hard time crediting the theory that enemies are indispensable to the way we define ourselves, that they reinforce our identity through a sort of permanent war. I've never felt that need: enemies have never given me anything but anxiety, and I would gladly go without them.

On the other hand, there's no doubt that the history of the human race is a history of enmities, and one can't eliminate the problem with a shrug. Enmities that can be ascribed to a particular motive frighten but don't excite me: the possession of a spring, of oil wells, of a region—those end in murder, war, slaughter and inspire horror.

I feel similarly about the animosities of daily life—those which arise from a slight, a trivial word, a bit of gossip, a promise not kept. Sometimes we regret them, sometimes we apologise, but in vain. I have to confess, I find any tension that can be traced back to trivial motives intolerable.

The only kind of enmity that interests me has no motivation, and can be summarised like this: "What did she do to you?" "I don't know, but the mere sight of her gets on my nerves." Here I think it's worth the effort to dig, partly because antipathy is an inadequate word, explaining almost nothing. What happens to our bodies when we bump into one another? Why do certain people seem to us so different that we can't accept them, can't recognise their humanity? Would a little goodwill remove any reason for hostility?

I know stories of completely unmotivated rejections, which just for that reason are fascinating. In particular I'm curious about relationships—between men, between women, between men and women—that begin with mutual interest and respect. These two people are comfortable together; there is curiosity, there is goodwill. It may not be the start of a friendship, but of something pleasant at least. Then there are some embarrassments, a little annoyance; suddenly a kind of smoke appears that burns the eyes and throat. Something is no longer working, but it's not easily identifiable, until one of them says: "That's it, I'd rather not see you any more," and the relationship breaks off.

A sympathetic closeness is transformed into a hostile distance. These two people hurt each other whenever possible, and for no reason that can be put into words. I suspect there's something in this type of situation that, if described completely, would allow us to take some steps forward. An enemy may simply be someone who, out of a sort of emotional exhaustion, has avoided the effort, the complexity, the pleasure—all the ambiguities of friendship.

# Creative Freedom

*6 October 2018*

I would never say to a woman director, "This is my book, this is my perspective. If you want to make a film, you have to stick to it." I wouldn't say anything, even if she systematically betrayed my text, even if she wanted to use it simply as a launch pad for her own creative impulse.

That's what I thought when Maggie Gyllenhaal, an actor I love, announced that she would adapt a novel of mine, *The Lost Daughter*, for the screen. I'm attached to that book in a particular way. I know that, with it, I ventured into dangerous waters without a life preserver. And part of me would like the story in Gyllenhaal's images to adhere faithfully to my story, to never go outside the perimeter I drew.

But my less primitive self knows that there's something much more important at stake than this instinct to protect my own inventions. Another woman has found in that text good reason to test her creative capacities. Gyllenhaal has decided, that is, to give cinematic

85

form not to my experience of the world but to hers, starting from *The Lost Daughter*.

It's important for me—for her, for all women—that her work be hers and turn out well. Mine already exists, with its strengths and defects. In the great warehouse of the arts, set up mainly by men, women have for a relatively short time been seeking the means and opportunities to give a form of their own to what they have learned from life. So I don't want to say: you have to stay inside the cage that I constructed. We've been inside the male cage for too long—and now that that cage is collapsing, a woman artist has to be absolutely autonomous. Her search shouldn't encounter obstacles, especially when it's inspired by the work, by the thought, of other women.

Being co-opted into the long, authoritative tradition created by men should not be the cost of making art. The stakes are higher: women have to contribute to an artistic genealogy of our own that stands up—in terms of intelligence, refinement, skill, richness of invention, emotional density—to the male tradition. In other words, we need to emphasise the force of our works—a force that is increasingly asserting itself, and profoundly modifying the sensibility of even the best men.

There is nothing wrong with a man wanting to make a film from my books: in fact, it is a positive sign. But in that case, I would tend not to be acquiescent. Even if he had a strongly defined vision of his own, I would ask him to respect my view, to adhere to my world, to enter the cage of my story without trying to drag it into his. It will do him more good, perhaps, than me.

# Plants

I love plants. Maybe even more than animals, more than cats, which I adore. I like everything about plants, but I always feel as though I know nothing. I buy them at the nursery, I distribute them on balconies and in every room, I plant them in the ground in the garden. I learn their names, including the scientific ones, and I write down in a notebook how much to water them, when to give them hormones, whether they need a lot of sun or a little.

And not only that: I study the types of soil, the time for pruning and the techniques. I worry about late freezes as if they were earth-quakes or tidal waves.

I take such care of my plants that I become fond of them. I check them continuously, I feel the soil with my fingers to see if it's still damp or dry. Out of love for them, I tolerate the unpleasant smell of organic fertilisers and the crowds of flies. I patiently rescue leaves attacked by parasites. And when I realise that one is mortally ill, I discover that I love it more than all the others and turn to trusted experts to find out what to do.

But while I have taught myself so much, I continue to think I am shamefully ignorant and that my ignorance will be punished. I feel that plants are alive, very alive, and yet prisoners. They can't move, they can't seek shelter, they can't escape clippers, hatchets, saws. They inspire pity and so I feel they are designated victims—an emblem, perhaps, of all the victims on this planet.

But a precisely opposite feeling is grafted on to my sense of pity. Their expansion worries me. They are prisoners and yet they extend, twist, creep their way in, break the stone. Their roots grow deeper and deeper; they try to send them elsewhere. Maybe it's that contrast that disorients me; they have in themselves a blind force that doesn't fit with their cheerful colours, their pleasing scents. At the first opportunity, they manage to get back everything that was taken from them, dissolving the shapes that we have imposed by domesticating them.

At the movies, on television, images of burning forests cause me as much suffering—I feel the life that's evaporating, hissing, writhing amid the flames—as the speeded-up images of tree sap, that like a cancer slides past every possible obstacle, frighten me.

At times I suspect that I devote myself to plants in this way because I'm afraid of them. But then I should admit I've assigned to vegetation a symbolism that applies to any form of life. We appreciate it, we love it—until, bursting the boundaries that our authority has set, it overflows.

# Leave-Taking

*20 October 2018*

I belong to that category of people who, after a dinner, after a party, are the last to leave. It's hard to say why—it's not clear even to me. I know that my hosts are tired and would like to go to sleep. I'm well aware that, even if I left right away, it would still take them an hour or so to straighten things up and get ready for bed. Yet I continue to ask questions and wait for answers—in short, to keep the conversation going. I don't do it because the evening has been especially pleasant and I want to prolong it. I'm not generally very sociable on occasions like this; I join conversations timidly and am quite sure that, after an hour, anyone can read in my face that I'm tired, falling asleep.

I deduce from this that my problem is leave-taking itself. I don't like to separate from people; even in the most superficial relationships, separating seems like a blast of cold air. I suppose I feel the anguish of loss. But what am I losing?

I've seen other people who, like me, tend to linger, but for reasons more obvious than mine. They're brilliant, they enjoy having an audience, they won't accept that the party's over and there's no more centre to occupy. Or they're the type who is always a little worried, who generally feels somewhat isolated, kept outside the circle of the hosts' intimate friends. They can't make up their minds and leave because they don't want to think that the party will continue, that the closer friends are just getting comfortable and will gossip about the ones who have left.

I'm not like that. Maybe, on a more banal level, the threshold scares me. What is waiting on the other side—something terrible? Or, worse still, nothing? I say to myself: I'm here, now, with people I somehow or other know, who somehow or other know me, but outside I will be alone with myself, with this tired body, with this voice locked in my head. And so I dawdle, I get up, I sit down again, I examine an object I had no interest in before.

But there's no need to think about some brooding inner tension. I'm pretty well, as usual; I'm simply lingering. I help tidy up, I become a little more talkative than when the other guests were here. I suddenly feel like telling the hosts about myself, inventing things if I don't want to be too revealing, listening to their confidences in return, touching an arm, a hand.

Maybe the truth is that saying goodbye seems to me a rejection of human warmth—even the minimal warmth that makes us feel solitude less. I mean real solitude, which rises up by surprise and lasts a few seconds, the solitude that derives not from lack of company or affection, but from our innate separateness from one another.

# Women Who Write

*27 October 2018*

Do men learn from women? Often. Do they admit it publicly? Rarely, even today. Let's stick to literature. No matter how hard I try, I can't think of many male writers who have said that they were in any way indebted to the work of a woman writer. Among Italians only one comes to mind, Giuseppe Tomasi di Lampedusa, the author of *The Leopard*, who wrote that he had benefitted from reading Virginia Woolf. I could list quite a few great male writers who either belittle their female colleagues, or attribute to them a capacity only to write banal, trifling stories—of marriage, children, love affairs; cheap romances and sentimental novels.

Recently, things have been changing, but not very much. For example, when some renowned male writer says in private, or in public, that we women writers are good, I would like to ask: are we as good as you, better than you, or good only within the context of books written by women? That is, have we broken out of the literary women's space we are confined to (and not only by the market)? Or have we overturned literature in general and its values?

In other words, if you are a male writer who reads me and finds me good, are you paying me a generous compliment of the sort paid to a female student who has learned her lesson well? Or are you willing to admit that, today, you can learn from writing by women as much as we women have learned—and are learning, reading over the centuries—from writing by men?

Here, in my opinion, things get complicated. Plenty of cultivated men are willing to praise us for our capacity to stir the emotions (and what does a woman do well, traditionally, if not stir the emotions and make the hours pass pleasantly?). But these men keep for themselves the literature that revolutionises, that ventures into minefields, that digs into political confrontation or addresses heroic struggles with power. The courage to go through the world fighting with words and deeds, street by street, remains in many people's imagination the province of male intellectuals. Women, meanwhile, are still assigned to the balcony, from where they may contemplate life passing by and describe it in tremulous words.

Many women who write, in every part of the world, in every field, do so with lucidity, with a pitiless gaze, with courage, with no concession to sentimentality. A widespread female intelligence that produces writing of a high literary quality has become manifest. But the cliche dies hard: we are emotional; we please. Men make great literature and teach fearlessly, through their words and deeds, how all the evil in the world should yield to good.

# Stereotyped

*3 November 2018*

Stereotypes are crude simplifications, but generally they don't lie. If I say that Italians eat spaghetti, it is not a lie; I'm simply reducing a complex reality, with its great cultural tradition, to a plate of pasta eaten by someone with a Sicilian cloth cap on his head. I do the same with, let's say, Americans, eaters of grilled steak in cowboy hats, or the English, bowler-hatted drinkers of tea as soon as the clock strikes five. All in all, there is nothing wrong with simplifying: simplification is like a first glance into a crowded hall, or a child's drawing of Mamma and Papa. The problem arises when we don't know that these are stereotypes, crude constructions, full of prejudice, and take them for reality.

The stories we tell traditionally make great use of stereotypes, whether they report facts that really happened or come from the imagination. Scornfully dismissing them as such isn't helpful. If we want to elevate and ennoble these stereotyped situations, these stereotyped characters, we could say that they somewhat resemble the narratives of fairytales. Without recourse to these, no story would flow, orally or in writing, in the theatre, in film, on television.

In fact, a story comes especially easily when the narrator doesn't even know that he's using proven formulas: the wolf and the lamb, the devil and the good god, the corrupt and the honest, the hero and the traitor, the king and the queen, beauty and the beast. The same is true of stereotypes, especially if we don't perceive their nature, feel their crudeness—which happens when we draw on our own lives and are convinced that our stories perfectly reflect reality.

It's useless to point out to the storyteller that stereotypes are abundant in real life. The narrator says he's sorry: look, the thief really *was* Neapolitan, and there really *was* laundry hanging in the alley.

More complex, on the other hand, is the conscious use of stereotypes to form a story that's purely entertaining; it requires great skill and expertise. In this case stereotypes become functional; the writer obeys rules; the story is a journey with inevitable stopping points—very familiar, yet always enjoyable.

It's a risk, in the end, to start from stereotypical situations and characters, and then to push them. This can succeed or not; it's like writing from inside the condition we find ourselves in every day. Don't we, in fact, orient ourselves in the world according to convenient generalisations, prejudices we take for independent judgments? And isn't it up to us, sooner or later, to try to confront this reality, which becomes knowable only if we venture at our own peril outside the frame?

The work is good when, from the cocoon of the stereotype, we manage to get at real life—which, because it's real life, darts unpredictably in every direction and can never be contained.

## The Book and the Film  *10 November 2018*

    I speak as an inexperienced screenwriter. When I write a book, and someone decides to make it into a movie, I'm glad.

    Then? Then the work begins. My first impression is traumatic, as the literary cover is torn off my novel by the screenwriters. It's a terrible moment: I worked on that text for years, and now everything seems to become impoverished: places, events, characters. A city square minutely described is reduced in the screenplay to the simple common noun: square. An event to which I devoted many pages shrinks, becomes a stage direction. Characters become names, actions are abridged, as are lines of dialogue. Stripped down, the novel suddenly appears to the writer to be a trick of literary words, a fraud, and she is slightly ashamed. The story, in this summary form, is banal. The density I thought I had achieved has vanished. I have to acknowledge that I failed to include things that now seem essential and gave too much space to what now seems superfluous. I want to say, "Let's give it up—my novel doesn't seem suitable."

Then, little by little, one gets used to writing for the screen; it's a functional type of writing, preparing the leap from the novel to the new work: the film. I calm down: my book is still fine; it contains what I had to write and was able to; it's sitting on the table, completely self-sufficient. But the film isn't there yet: it wants to be, and relies on cinematic writing, whose job is to identify the film's requirements and satisfy them. The perimeter is drawn by my book, but inside that perimeter, everything is rearranged, reimagined based on the show—the real objective. Only at this point is the imagination kindled.

I can see very clearly what, while I was writing the book, was either overexplained or confused. I feel the need for scenes that in my story would have been superfluous. I write dialogue that the tone of my text wouldn't tolerate. I often seem to be collaborating on "remaking" my novel, with writing that I would never have used. And when it all seems in order—the story and the dialogues flow; we've honed, eliminated—the work seems finished.

Yet this is just the beginning, a preliminary goal for writing that, on the one hand, reduces the book to its skeleton, and on the other still displays the features of every written word: ambiguity, openness to multiple representations. In the film or television version, everything, absolutely everything, will have to have a precise aspect: the streets, the church, the tunnel, the houses, the rooms, a classroom, the desks. And everyone, absolutely everyone, will have to have a particular body.

This inevitable definition of every detail will happen outside the screenplay itself. As for the book, it will stay behind, imperturbable, while the film comes closer and closer to one of its possible incarnations.

# Dying Young

*17 November 2018*

A woman I was very attached to died young, at thirty-eight. She had been married to a man she loved, had three small children and many talents that were beginning to bear fruit. I was younger than she was when she died; now, I'm much older. For a long time I considered her thirty-eight years a sort of goal. If that had been her allotted span, surely that limit could also be mine. So I thought of my life as if it would not last longer than thirty-eight years.

I know that may seem ridiculous but, in some corner of myself, it really was like that. And, all in all, I'm glad: in many ways I had a different sense of time from my contemporaries. I ran; they lingered. I felt old and burdened by responsibilities; they seemed young and irresponsible.

I always felt that I didn't have enough time. I went to bed late, got up early, and used any idle moment—between children, work, marital disasters—to mould myself as quickly as possible, so that I would be able to say: this is me, these are my abilities. My contemporaries seemed to have infinite time ahead of them.

But there was more. I lived with an anomalous sense of what it is to be old, of death. For example, I used to feel an irritation that even I found unreasonable when I heard someone say, "He died young, he was sixty-four." To me, sixty-four was the age of Methuselah, an excess, an abuse. Or maybe, in some way, an insult to my friend, her husband, her children.

When I got to thirty-eight, however, things gradually changed. I was pleased that I had made it and thought, "Everything after this is a bonus."

And without realising it, I began to slow down. The years accumulated, one after another and, looking back, I seemed to have lived too intensely, demanded too much from myself and from others. I started feeling guilty. Had I bitten into life more greedily than my friend?

Not only that: with every year that passed, I felt relief, or even satisfaction, as if I'd won a contest, as if I were speeding miraculously towards some goal that was there only for me. Time slipped away, and every moment seemed one I wasn't entitled to. I felt like a thief and, at the same time, experienced the pleasure of the kleptomaniac.

Today, I think of my friend as a person miraculously complete, and that makes me happy—it moves me. I'm still waiting, though more and more indifferently, for a new episode.

# Jealousy

*24 November 2018*

To my regret, I frequently come across jealous people. In my fiction, I've written often about this repugnant feeling but, in general, unhappily. The result is always disappointing: from Shakespeare to Proust, everything that could be said has been said, beautifully, and it seems a wasted effort. Besides, I feel some reluctance to dig into myself and what I know about the many jealous people I've loved and love. Not to mention that I often run into people who say, in anguished tones, "Forget it, you don't know enough about jealousy. I do, I know all the torments." Jealousy is a yellowish muck that we stick our hands into without even the satisfaction of extracting some truth of our own.

And yet it's hard to ignore the feeling: like it or not, in trivial or extreme form, we've all experienced it—not necessarily in love, but in every kind of relationship. Of course I've met many people who swear they are not the jealous type. But I've pretty quickly had to put them into the category of perjurers: jealousy suddenly appeared in their eyes, though they hurried to retract it—embarrassed, hoping I hadn't noticed.

It's mainly the cultured who are careful to hide their jealousy, because they feel that deep down this is a petty but significant presumption: their intolerance of the fact that the people they love may feel pleasure without them, in the company of others. The jealous person wants to be the only source of the beloved's wellbeing. And yet, as we know, the press of life is so strong, so fiercely expansive, that it can't be completely fulfilled by one relationship; all of us are tempted to risk even the most solid bonds when attracted by others.

If we maintain some clear-headedness and a little self-control, we can see that a large part of the beloved's existence inevitably takes place outside the enclosure in which we want to place him. To keep watch is impossible; every attack of jealousy underlines our condition as a frail human being—we're not indispensable, we're afraid of abandonment—and is degrading; it takes away our aura. And for that reason, we try desperately to contain our jealous rages. At times, we even manage to transform them into an impulse to give the other all the attention, all the kindness, all the understanding we're capable of.

It's an exercise that doesn't always succeed, partly because the beloved seems to think it's intended to demonstrate—not only in private, but publicly—that we are not enough. The moment the inevitable feeling of inadequacy prevails, along with the impossibility of making oneself the sole purpose of another's life, there is no way out. We shut the beloved up in a cage, preferring that he die spiritually and even physically—rather than expose us to the humiliating wound of his escape.

## Not Enough

The age-old discussion of talent hasn't made great advances, as far as I know. It's just as it was in the ancient world: there are some who say that poets are born, not made; and there are some who claim that a natural inclination is useful but not sufficient—that if you want to achieve something good, it has to be cultivated.

I belong to the ranks of those who adhere to the second notion, which is as old as Cicero and Quintilian. Talent is insufficient: if it's not cultivated, it ends up, in the best cases, inventing the wheel, only to discover that this has been done already. Those who feel they have an artistic vocation have an obligation not to squander it by being content with what pours from their heart. The heart is fine; but in order not to waste one's creativity, it's even better to learn from tradition, to appropriate techniques developed over time; not to go where the wind blows, but to choose models, a proper poetic genealogy from which to draw energy and ambition.

Does this mean that anyone who has a little talent and a degree from some school or academy attesting to a good education is bound for great things? I'm afraid not. It means only that a person who feels an urgent need to give adequate form to his own experience has the right and the duty to do so—if possible, without becoming the bore who tugged on Horace's tunic, begging him to read his poems.

Great artists are not born and probably not made. There is something more mysterious that intervenes without warning and acts on talent, whether raw or cultivated, in an always surprising way. This is luck. The poet, unfortunately, has to have not only the gift of talent, not only the privilege and the culture of being able to nurture and refine it. The poet also has to be lucky.

He has to have the kind of luck with which we tend to justify someone else's success, when we can't find some more demeaning explanation. But in what sense? We can work all our lives with discipline and intelligence and skill to give shape to our world, and never make a significant breakthrough. Luck is that breakthrough—the stunning moment when our own very individual and yet very limited work is transformed: let's say, from a journey to the other world to the *Divine Comedy*, from a seafaring adventure to *Moby-Dick*.

Unfortunately, nothing can assure us—not criticism, not success, not even ourselves—that that sudden breakthrough was really there or permanent. The future of any work is even more obscure than our own. We have to resign ourselves to that fact and work with stubborn dedication all our lives, without asking for anything more.

# The Female Version

*8 December 2018*

Sometimes I play a game with myself in which I take stories with male protagonists—famous stories that I like a lot—and ask myself: if the protagonist were a woman, would it work just as well? Could Melville's Bartleby, for example, be female? Or Stevenson's Jekyll? Italo Svevo's Zeno? Calvino's Baron in the Trees?

For many years, the game has revolved mainly around Wakefield, a short story by Nathaniel Hawthorne. Wakefield is a man who lives in crowded 19th-century London. One morning, he says goodbye to his wife and goes out. He's supposed to be away for a few days; he doesn't leave the city, but instead, for no reason, with no plan, he goes to live near his own house, and for twenty years—until, in the same impulsive way, he returns to his wife—confines himself to observing his own absence. The story is well known and much studied.

What if Wakefield were a woman instead of a man, a wife instead of a husband? Once, I even tried to maul poor Hawthorne by rewriting the story that way, but I quickly got stuck: something wasn't working. I'm not sure I understood what the problem was. There are plenty of stories, true or invented, about women who all of a sudden leave home, abandoning everything; evidently the issue isn't that. And it doesn't seem to be in the return home, either—although, in my experience, a woman who decides to give it all up rarely turns back, while men generally, at a certain point, need their Ithaca. (I know numerous couples who have got back together after one or even two decades, and he is the one who proposes it—especially when old age peeks in, along with the fear of illness and death.) A female Wakefield falters, I'm afraid, right at the heart of things, at its darkest, most mysterious and hence finest moment.

When you have to imagine a woman who, for no reason, abandons everything and for twenty years lives near her family, meets them on the street, sees them suffer, observes them as they change physically, yet doesn't go back, the story flounders. The Wakefield who is present and absent like an idle divinity, simply watching, without intervening, seems to me inevitably male.

And yet the situation that Hawthorne developed still attracts me—the impassive surveillance, the indifferent proximity. Sometimes, I think that it's only cliches about the feminine that make us consider certain behaviours essentially masculine. Today, a female Wakefield might go further than the male Wakefield. Maybe, emphasising the absurdity of being absent and at the same time present, she would dig more deeply into a contradiction that is well known to her: the need for the other—and the necessity of separating from him.

# Poetry and Prose

*15 December 2018*

I grew up with the idea that being a poet is for truly exceptional people, while anyone can have a go at prose. Maybe it was the fault of my school, which instilled a sort of awe for anyone who writes poetry. Schoolbooks and teachers portrayed poets as superior beings, with great virtues and sometimes fascinating vices; they were in permanent dialogue with the gods, thanks to the Muses—able to look at past and future as no one else did, and naturally they had an exceptional talent for language. I found this paralysing, and so at a certain point I reduced their status in my mind. But I became an assiduous reader of poetry.

I love the connections poetry makes, so unexpected and bold that they become indecipherable. I'm sure that writing mediocre poems is a mortal sin; if people still mainly told their stories in verse, as they did for many centuries, I would be too embarrassed to write. But even if, after a long battle, prose now occupies almost all the narrative space, deep inside I feel that it's a constitutionally inferior form of writing. This is probably what has driven me since I was a girl to exaggerate with language; part of me aspires to the poetic and hates the prosaic—I want to prove that I'm not inferior.

But writing prose with the rhythm, the harmony, the images that characterise a poem is a death trap. What in verse can give form to a dazzling truth, in prose becomes the falsest of affectations. The sentence takes on a rhythmic cadence, the words and images are sentimental, the need to avoid the ordinary leads to bizarre formulations and artificial expressions. It's as if the writer believes that aiming for some kind of poetic truth means the prose has to become lyrical. It took me—a slave to good poetry, but incapable of making it—a long time to understand that. I strove for writing that was lofty, vigorous, full of ostentatious verbal inventions.

Then I said to myself that poetry—or, if you prefer, beauty—should be achieved line by line, through the medium of prose—that is, keeping strictly to a form of expression that is effective and clear. It's an easy plan to make, but a hard and laborious one to put into practice. I go back and forth. Today I am self-indulgent, tomorrow I am self-punishing—and I am never happy with the results. Through a fear of making everything too lyrical, I compose cold, inexpressive sentences. Out of exhaustion, I return to the rough draft with all its sloppiness, rather than settle for yet another beautiful, refined, unbearably artificial version.

The urge to make every line a marvel is strong. The only thing I seem to have learned is to throw away the page that dazzles with its style—and thus obscures the portrayal of nature and human endeavour.

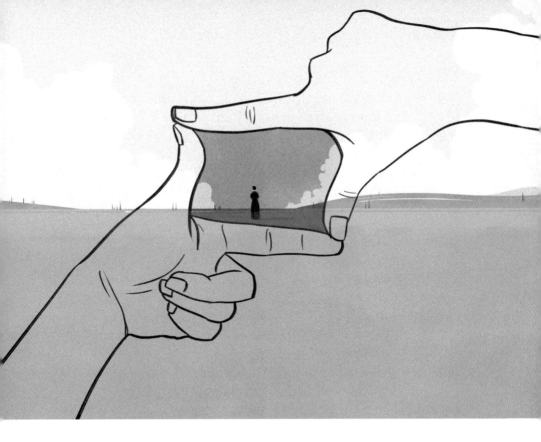

## This Is Me                           *22 December 2018*

I am one of those people who never like the way they look in photographs or videos. As soon as I realise that a friend or relative is pointing a phone at me, I turn my back, cover my face with my hands, and say, "No, I'll look bad, stop it, I'm not photogenic." But some time ago I happened to find a photo of myself at seventeen, and I liked it so much that—extraordinarily—I had it framed and put it on display on a bookshelf. Everyone—friends, relatives—who saw it was puzzled: how pretty you look, is that really you? Even a person who's known me for decades and is very fond of me said, after praising the image, "But to tell you the truth, I don't think you really looked like that."

Eventually, I, too, had to admit that I liked this picture precisely because I didn't at all resemble the image I usually had of myself. Was it possible that I had had those features only at seventeen, at the end of a painful adolescence (like almost every adolescence)? Hard to say. When I think about that year, it doesn't seem to me that I was especially satisfied with myself, or with my appearance, something that the photo would have justified. Rather, I had to admit that at the time the image hadn't particularly struck me—maybe I considered it just one of the many I would happily have torn up. Or probably I hadn't disliked the photo, but, because I didn't have a high opinion of myself, I hadn't recognised myself and had immediately forgotten it.

Had I looked like that only in the fraction of a second in which the shot was taken? Was there something wrong with the camera? Was that image an invention of the device? But then, how had I reached the point, today, of framing and displaying it? Did I want, in this phase of my life, to deceive myself, to remember myself as I had never been?

It seems to me that I found the answer this morning, writing. A "me" was photographed that does in fact exist, but which doesn't coincide with what I normally was and am. It's a "me" showing off the best of myself, thus escaping my usual physical appearance. And I don't think it's just me who experiences this—it can happen to anyone. It's the very rare moment when, after successfully getting through an ordeal, after a courageous gesture, after some miraculously creative act, we say to ourselves, in amazement and satisfaction: "I would never have believed I was capable of that." It's the moment when everyone—even the camera—says to us: "Ah, how well you look today." A different "I" is released, happy in every cell, and so even our face is different.

Then, like an aquatic divinity that is visible for only a few seconds, we are swallowed up, to return to our everyday aspect.

# Black Skies

*29 December 2018*

As a child I loved storms, and as an adult, too, I've felt an excitement in the presence of dark skies, lightning, thunder, the rushing sound of water, puddles, the smell of wet clothes. I also like fine weather, but for me the smell of the air before the rain has something more.

Whenever it rained, my mother had endless warnings. She was afraid I'd catch a cold, she bundled me up till I was almost suffocating, she worried about wet feet. But I dreamed of splashing with my feet in the rain water; I wanted to feel my hair pasted to my head, the drops sliding into my eyes. As a child and adolescent, I experienced rain as a promise of adventure—the exposure of the body to the wild, a challenge to the swelling, threatening sky. And as a woman I loved spring; I'd happily lie in the sun, but I adored autumn, too, even the arrival of the cold. I never worried about weather: heat, humidity, wind, rain, snow, cold—the more I was outside, the better.

The seasons were time running pleasantly in a circle, like a happy dog chasing its tail.

A few decades ago, out of curiosity, I began to read about climate change. At first it seemed a kind of reactionary pessimism: increase in the greenhouse effect, global warming, rising ocean temperatures, melting glaciers, the end of the world on the horizon. I read in my usual way, wanting to understand and form an opinion, but also to fantasise. In fact I didn't understand much, I didn't fantasise much. Was it possible the ultimate devastation of the planet was among the many devastations caused by the human race? Was it possible the animal man, that infinitesimal piece of nature, in the course of his brief history had managed to irreversibly damage all the rest?

As a girl I learned that, while progress was unlimited, not many enjoyed its fruits. Yet if the means of production and consumption could be straightened out, things would advance in a just manner. What we learn when we're young is difficult to correct. So for a while I calmed myself, by embracing the opinion that climate change had always been there and that man had very little to do with its latest manifestations. All very wrong: I kept reading, and I repented.

And now I've become obsessive. I repeat to friends and relatives: the sea level is rising, the ice is melting, greenhouse gases are increasing, the atmosphere is warming, and it's our fault, the fault of the way of life and production imposed on us: it has to be changed immediately. Mainly, though, my lighthearted pleasure in the seasons has disappeared. Now I hate these eternal summers, I'm afraid of the furious heat that starts early and won't end. And the black skies with the rain cascading down terrify me, making streets into rivers, burying people and things under the mud.

## Stories That Instruct

*5 January 2019*

There's a very old function of literature that over time has lost currency, probably because of its dangerous proximity to the political and ethical spheres. I mean the idea that one of the purposes of a text is to instruct. Over the past fifty years, we have wisely convinced ourselves that the pleasure and enjoyment of a text are at one with its style. Very true: a text is made up of words, and the more beautifully chosen and put together the words are, the more seductive the text, and the more disruptive to the body of the reader. But the words, delighting us, shape our visions of the world; they penetrate our bodies, flow in and alter it, educating our gaze, feelings, even our position on different issues. Besides giving pleasure, style, in accordance with a long tradition, moves and teaches us.

We fall in love with a text partly for the way it unwittingly informs us; that is, for the wealth of vivid, true experiences that pass from the writer directly into the life of the reader. It's not just the meticulous choice of vocabulary, the metaphors, the memorable similes. What counts is how the writer inserts herself into the literary tradition—not only with her ability to orchestrate words, but with her ideas and the very personal store of urgent things she has to tell. An individual talent acts like a fishing net that captures daily experiences, holds them together imaginatively, and connects them to fundamental questions about the human condition.

So style really is all, but in the sense that the more powerful it is, the more material it holds for comprehensive life lessons. Note, however, that I'm not alluding to novels that use literature to deal with vital contemporary subjects: world hunger, the threat of new fascisms, terrorism, religious conflicts, racism, sexuality, digitisation and its effects, and so on. I have nothing against such books; in fact, I'm eager to read them. Gripping stories can be full of science or sociology that shines a light on the various catastrophes that threaten the planet; ideologies are disseminated, theses sustained, political battles joined.

But when I talk about instruction I don't mean that kind of book. I'm not thinking of a didactic, moralising literature. I'm just trying to say that every work of value is also a transmission of firsthand knowledge—knowledge that is unexpected and, especially, hard to reduce to a form that is not literary. I mean learning that is pleasurable, learning that changes us inwardly—dramatically, even—under the impact of words that are true and charged with feeling.

## The Last Time

*12 January 2019*

This exercise ends here: I gave myself a year, and the year is up. I had never done work like this, and I hesitated a good deal before trying it. I was afraid of the weekly deadline; I was afraid of having to write even if I didn't feel like it; I was afraid of the need to publish without having scrupulously considered every word. In the end, curiosity won out.

I tried to meet the challenge by imagining that I had to answer fifty-two questions in writing, one a week. I thought that was something I knew how to do by now: for years, I'd been answering journalists' questions. So that's how I proceeded, diligently. But I have to admit that, despite the extreme courtesy of my editors, I was constantly afraid of not succeeding in the task I'd undertaken, of somehow rashly being insulting to readers, of losing faith in myself and having to give up. Fortunately, the anxiety of publication was amply counterbalanced by the pleasure of writing. Today I can say with assurance that, even if I never have this experience again, it was very useful to me, and I'm grateful to the *Guardian* for giving me the opportunity.

I have written as an author of novels, taking on matters that are important to me and that—if I have the will and the time—I'd like to develop within real narrative mechanisms. I think I left out only one feeling among those that interest me, but only because it sustained my last book and it seemed excessive to return to it: I'm talking about inequality, about the disasters that it wreaks on an economic, social and cultural level. Everything about these times, I have to say, worries me, but that the majority of the human race— women, children, men—is subjected in various ways to the effects of inequality seems to me at the core of all the problems that consume us. Above all, inequality generates an extraordinary waste of minds and creative energies, which, if they were trained and put to use, would likely make our history an active laboratory for repairing the damage we've caused so far—or at least of controlling its effects, rather than an unbearable list of horrors.

I'd like to thank the people who have had the patience to translate my texts into English (Ann Goldstein), to verify their coherence, suggest cuts or additions, give them titles (Melissa Denes), and illustrate them with imagination and intelligence and humour (Andrea Ucini). I'd especially like to thank those who have been kind enough to read them. Before this, I was used to the rhythm of book publication, to a novel's compactness and autonomy. If my books went to the book shop, they met readers; for a while, I would experience the anxiety of being their author, but then I went on with my life, often for years, distancing myself as far as possible from the torment of a new publication. Writing this column has instead made me tense every Saturday. It has been the permanent exposure of fragments of myself; I couldn't free myself from one before I had to think about the next. Luckily, yes, there were readers—rightly either welcoming or hostile. I am indebted to all of them—few, many—who, agreeing or disagreeing, connected with these brief trickles of ink.

**Elena Ferrante** is the author of *The Days of Abandonment* (Europa, 2005), *Troubling Love* (Europa, 2006), *The Lost Daughter* (Europa, 2008) and the international best-selling novel in four instalments known as the Neapolitan Quartet (*My Brilliant Friend, The Story of a New Name*, *Those Who Leave and Those Who Stay,* and *The Story of the Lost Child*, Europa 2012-2015). She is also the author of *Frantumaglia: A Writer's Journey* and a children's picture book illustrated by Mara Cerri, *The Beach at Night*.

**Ann Goldstein** has translated into English all of Elena Ferrante's books, including each of the *New York Times* best-selling instalments in Ferrante's Neapolitan Quartet, the fourth of which, *The Story of the Lost Child*, was shortlisted for the MAN Booker International Prize. She has been honoured with a Guggenheim Fellowship and is a recipient of the PEN Renato Poggioli Translation Award. She lives in New York.

**Andrea Ucini** is a self-taught illustrator, born and raised in Italy and now living in the countryside of Hundested, Denmark, near Copenhagen, with his wife, three children and plenty of animals. He works in a studio surrounded by nature and the changing seasons.